BEST IN SHOW

Gerald S. Binks

Best in Show

BREEDING AND EXHIBITING BUDGERIGARS

ARCO PUBLISHING, INC.
NEW YORK

Published 1985 by Arco Publishing, Inc.
215 Park Avenue South, New York, NY 10003

First published 1974

Library of Congress Cataloging in Publication Data

Binks, Gerald S.
    Best in show.

    Includes index.
    1. Budgerigars.   2. Budgerigars – Breeding.
3. Budgerigars – Exhibitions.   I. Title.
SF473.B8B56 1985   636.6'864   84–9349
ISBN 0–668–06282–7

Printed in Great Britain

Contents

Foreword

It is a long time since a really comprehensive book on the budgerigar was published. Gerald Binks has had many years of experience in the keeping and breeding of this attractive bird and is therefore able to write on the subject with extensive practical knowledge.

This book covers all aspects of housing, general management, feeding and health problems. It also gives much help for the breeding season, with its attendant difficulties, and many hints to ensure success on the showbench. The beginner in the hobby will find everything he needs to know and the champion breeder will also read it with interest.

MARGERY KIRKBY-MASON

Seaton, Devon

Preface

Budgerigar breeding and showing has become so popular throughout the United Kingdom that today British budgerigars lead the world for quality. Breeders, by their skill and imagination, have achieved such a high standard that those in other countries now eagerly seek British stock to introduce into their studs. Keeping birds used to be referred to as the 'poor man's hobby'; these days nothing could be further from the truth, since Open Show winners can command substantial prices for their birds. However it is one aim of this book to assist both newcomers and established breeders who, like myself, have had to start without a deep pocket and work their way into Open Championship competition.

I had intended to write a book just on breeding and exhibiting, but I felt that this would result in the reader not understanding the hobby as a whole and so the book grew. It is impossible to include every detail in the space allowed and I have concentrated on the more important facts. I am not a geneticist and while I have included a chapter on this important science, there are many reference books available to supplement this. My aim has been to reduce the technical genetic terms to a minimum and concentrate on the points which I believe are the most important for budgerigar breeders. It must be admitted that the colour breeding of budgerigars is of interest to many, particularly beginners, who start by filling a decorative garden aviary with an assortment to please the eye. Some of these beginners become fascinated by the exhibition world and the pursuance of quality and if you fall into this category read on.

I have devoted almost thirty years to budgerigars as a breeder and exhibitor and my delight in breeding a winner is still as great today as it was when I started. Much of the pleasure I obtain is from the friends I have made in all parts of the world and I would emphasize I place that friendship before the birds themselves. I visit many shows and meetings every year and while this occupies much of my time it continues to give great personal satisfaction.

I must express my thanks to Miss Margery Kirkby-Mason for so kindly writing the Foreword; to the Budgerigar Society for their permission to quote their rules and regulations and to my typist Valerie Wilkinson for all her work. My appreciation also goes to my photographers Margery Kirkby-Mason, Sally Ann Thompson, Edward Finch and

Graham Clarke for their hours of patience with difficult subjects, and indeed to the following fanciers whose aviaries and stock appear in this book: M. G. Wheeler, C. D. Saunders, G. Clarke, Messrs Muir and Crossman, Messrs Ormerod and Sadler, Mr. and Mrs. J. J. Tidball and Miss M. Kirkby-Mason.

To Douglas and Elizabeth Peet my gratitude for their encouragement to start this book and thereby fulfil an ambition and, finally, to my family and my friends who have helped me with my hobby for thirty years, my heartfelt thanks.

GERALD S. BINKS

Tanglewood,
Knowle Grove,
Virginia Water,
Surrey.

1974

Introduction to the Budgerigar Society

The breeding of exhibition budgerigars is a combination of art and science, to which must be added a slice of luck and the irrepressible optimism of the stud owner. Few of us have been initiated into the hobby in the ideal way, usually having started with perhaps a single pet or a decorative garden aviary, the emphasis being on colour and the lively character of the budgerigars.

Once introduced to the exhibition world one becomes not a pet owner but a fancier and like many other hobbies it can occupy most of one's spare thinking time. The reason that the budgerigar has become so popular is that it is not too difficult to manage as a beginner, it is an increasing challenge to breed an outstanding bird for the showbench and as the breeder progresses he can acquire the occasional outcross to improve his exhibition successes still further. Budgerigars are very hardy and can exist in quite extreme temperatures, hence the fancy now has strong representation in Sweden and Canada, which is a far cry from its Australian origins.

The budgerigar was insignificant as an exhibition bird until 1925 when a group of dedicated fanciers formed The Budgerigar Society which is the main body of the budgerigar world. Any breeder who wants to become conversant with all aspects of the fancy should become a member immediately. He will receive his own personal code number which he is entitled to have engraved on the closed budgerigar rings purchased through the Society and he will receive four quarterly copies of the Society publication, the *Budgerigar Bulletin*. There are further advantages. When exhibiting at certain shows sponsored by The Budgerigar Society one is entitled to compete for rosettes, diplomas, spoon prizes and cash by quoting one's code number on the entry form.

The Society has a governing body of administrators, the General Council, which is voted into office annually and from which is chosen the Executive Committee. It is these two bodies which set the standards required in the Ideal Budgerigar, produce illustrations and formulate the show rules and scale of points referred to later in this book.

In addition to the main body, the country is divided up into geographical locations and Area Societies affiliated to the Budgerigar Society have been formed. These societies are listed below and the addresses of their current Secretaries may be obtained from either the

Budgerigar Society or *Cage and Aviary Birds*, a weekly publication where they are frequently advertised.

Lancashire, Cheshire and North Wales (including the Isle of Man) Budgerigar Society.
Lincolnshire and East Anglia Budgerigar and Foreign Bird Society.
London and Southern Counties Budgerigar Society.
Midland Budgerigar and Foreign Bird Association.
Northern Budgerigar Society.
South Midlands Budgerigar and Foreign Bird Society.
South Wales and Monmouthshire Budgerigar Society.
Western Counties Budgerigar and Foreign Bird Society.
Yorkshire Budgerigar Society.

Specialist Societies
Clearwing Budgerigar Breeders' Association.
Crested Budgerigar Club.
Variegated Budgerigar Club.

I would strongly recommend all fanciers to belong to both their Area Society and the Budgerigar Society from the moment they become interested in the hobby, in order to obtain full benefit from the literature and the prizes offered by the societies at shows in every part of the country. Affiliated to the Area Societies are the clubs which are found in towns and villages throughout the U.K.

This introductory information will be familiar to the established fanciers, but to the newcomer it will I hope be of assistance in understanding the structure of the Budgerigar Society and the part it plays in assisting every member.

THE BUDGERIGAR SOCIETY
welcomes new members

Enthusiasts in the United States wishing information may contact the American Budgerigar Society, 141 Hill Street Extension, Naugatuck, CN 06770. Corienne Traver, Secretary.

1. History of the Exhibition Budgerigar

Today's domesticated and exhibition budgerigar originated in the wild in the green form and is a native of Australia. The latin name for the genus is Melopsittacus undulatus and two sub species have been recorded, namely Melopsittacus undulatus intermedius from the Northern Territory and Melopsittacus undulatus pallidiceps from Western Australia. The western form is paler on the head and body while the northern sub species is paler on the neck and back. The name 'Budgerigar' is a corruption of the Australian Aboriginal name Betcherrygah, though it has a variety of other names; undulated grass parakeet, scallop parrot, zebra grass parakeet are but a few.

The distribution of budgerigars across the Australian continent is extremely wide because of their habit of migrating in large flocks to wherever the food and water is plentiful. However they chiefly inhabit the inland grass plains, not the coastal regions. They eat grass seeds and shoots, plantains and the buds of eucalyptus trees and scrub trees found in the immediate locality of the grasses. It is thought they also eat small forms of insect life. The main breeding grounds are situated east of Perth in Western Australia, where there is a variable rainfall which affects the density of their breeding, and in the western part of New South Wales and South Australia, principally the area traversed by the Murray River. The nests are made on a community basis, many pairs abounding in the same area, and are to be found in soft rotting wood bare of any nesting material. Any hole or hollow is utilized and the nests vary considerably in depth. The eggs number four to six and the incubation period is eighteen days. Several broods are produced by each pair but breeding stops as soon as the food and water conditions in the locality become adverse.

The first illustration of a budgerigar was published in 1805 by Shaw & Nodder and not until 1840 was the first record made of live specimens coming into the United Kingdom. These were brought over by the naturalist John Gould and it is recorded that a relative of Gould's, Charles Coxen, was the first to breed with them in captivity. From these first birds the Europeans have developed the bird to its present day magnificence.

In the process numerous colour mutations have occurred to give us a considerable range from which to choose. It is significant that neither red nor black body coloration has yet been achieved in budgerigars, whereas both these colours are widespread in other parrotlike species. From the wild greens, the yellow birds were quickly established and in 1881 the skyblue was reported in Holland. The first blues came to Great Britain from Belgium in 1910 and were exhibited in that year, when they caused a sensation. The late Allen Silver is quoted as re-calling the first white occurring in 1920 from a pair of skyblues bred by H. D. Astley.

The appearance in 1919 of greywing greens was followed by cobalts in 1923 and mauves in 1924. Greywing skyblues were recorded in 1928 and greywing cobalts and mauves in the two years that followed. At about this time the Japanese began to take great interest and even in those days were prepared to pay £50–£75 per bird for the blue and white series budgerigars. The record price paid was for a pair of prize winning cobalts which realized £200. These prices however were not sustained once the colours became commonplace and their value had dropped by the mid 1930s. The late Mrs. Brown of Morecambe imported the first recorded whitewing violet from Australia.

About 1932 the first albino mutations were recorded both in this country and Germany. The Germans managed to develop from these the lutino (a buttercup yellow bird with red eyes), and breeding of these colours continued rapidly. Clearwings and Australian greys appeared in 1935, as did opalines. Shortly after this an English form of grey was established which turned out to have recessive characteristics but this was quickly outstripped for quality by the Australian dominant grey. Regrettably the English recessive greys subsequently disappeared completely.

Denmark has the distinction of recording the first green and yellow pied strain, which did not arrive in the U.K. until 1948 when Cyril Rogers obtained a number of these birds from Herr C. af. Enehjelm, at that time the Director of the Helsinki Zoological Gardens. Quite suddenly, in 1937, the violet was recorded simultaneously in the U.K., Australia and Denmark. Since then very few mutations have occurred. We await the appearance of red or pink, or brown other than cinnamon, or black. The Budgerigar Information Bureau offers a £500 prize for the first genuine pink breasted budgerigar bred by a British breeder.

The Ideal Budgerigar

The Budgerigar Society has over the years produced a 'Standard' to which all breeders and judges are expected to conform; any deviations from this 'Standard' are regarded as faults. Basically the shape and deportment and head qualities of the exhibition bird are of paramount importance. Colour, while significant, is of secondary importance. As to size, the beginner will quickly appreciate that the 'Open Show Champion' specimens are enormous by pet standards and 'a good big one will always beat a good little one'. The Ideal Budgerigar is 8½ in. long from the top of the head to the end of the tail and to attain such a bird with every other factor in perfect order is the challenge all exhibitors face.

Below is the current Budgerigar Society Ideal Budgerigar Standard, along with the illustration issued to all members, plus the Society 'Scale of Points' which emphasizes those features regarded as significant for judging.

The Budgerigar Society's Standard for the Ideal Budgerigar

CONDITION is essential. If a bird is not in condition it should never be considered for any award.

TYPE – Gracefully tapered from nape of neck to tip of tail, with an approximately straight back line, and a rather deep nicely curved chest.

LENGTH – The ideal length is 8½ in. from the crown of the head to the tip of the tail. Wings well braced, carried just above the cushion of the tail and not crossed. The ideal length of the wing is 3¾ in. from the butt to the tip of the longest primary flight, which must contain seven visual primary flight feathers fully grown and not broken. *No bird showing 'long-flighted' characteristics shall be eligible to take any award.*

HEAD – Large, round, wide and symmetrical when viewed from any angle; curvature of skull commencing at cere, to lift outward and upward, continuing over the top and to base of head in one graceful sweep.

BEAK – Set well into face.

EYE – To be bold and bright, and positioned well away from front, top and back skull.

NECK – To be short and wide when viewed from either side or front.

WINGS – Approximately two-fifths the total length of the bird, well braced, carried just above the cushion of the tail and not crossed.

TAIL – To be straight and tight with two long tail feathers.

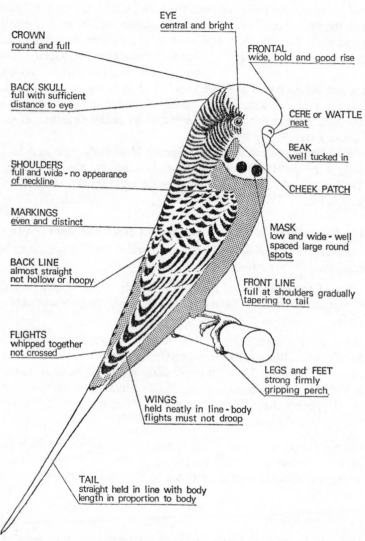

CROWN
round and full

EYE
central and bright

FRONTAL
wide, bold and good rise

BACK SKULL
full with sufficient
distance to eye

CERE or WATTLE
neat

BEAK
well tucked in

SHOULDERS
full and wide - no appearance
of neckline

CHEEK PATCH

MARKINGS
even and distinct

MASK
low and wide - well
spaced large round
spots

BACK LINE
almost straight
not hollow or hoopy

FRONT LINE
full at shoulders gradually
tapering to tail

FLIGHTS
whipped together
not crossed

LEGS and FEET
strong firmly
gripping perch.

WINGS
held neatly in line - body
flights must not droop

TAIL
straight held in line with body
length in proportion to body

The main features of a budgerigar
Reproduced by permission of the Budgerigar Society

POSITION – Steady on perch at an angle of 30 degrees from the vertical, looking fearless and natural.

MASK AND SPOTS – Mask to be clear, deep and wide, and where demanded by the Standard should be ornamented by six evenly spaced large round throat spots, the outer two being partially covered at the base by cheek patches, the size of the spots to be in proportion to the rest of the make-up of the bird as shown in the illustrated Ideal. Spots can be either too large or too small.

LEGS AND FEET – Legs should be straight and strong, and two front and two rear toes and claws firmly gripping perch.

MARKINGS – Wavy markings on cheek, head, neck, back and wings to stand out clearly.

COLOUR – Clear and level and of an even shade.

The Budgerigar Society's Scale of Points

REVISED SCALE OF POINTS **Remember: Condition is Supremely Important**	*Size shape balance and deportment*	*Size and shape of head*	*Colour*	*Mask and spots*	*Wing markings*
Green (Light, Dark or Olive)	45	20	15	15	5
Grey Green (Light, Medium or Dark) ..	45	20	15	15	5
Yellow (incldg. Op. Yell. but excldg. Lutino)	45	20	35	—	—
Olive Yellow (including Cinnamon Olive Yellow)	45	20	35	—	—
Skyblue, Cobalt, Mauve or Violet ..	45	20	15	15	5
Grey (Light, Medium or Dark)	45	20	15	15	5
White (Light Suffusion including Opaline White but excluding Albino)	45	20	*35	—	—
Whitewing (Skyblue, Cobalt, Mauve, Violet or Grey)	45	20	*35	—	—
Yellow-wing (Light, Dark, Olive or Grey Green)	45	20	*35	—	—
Greywing (Light, Dark, Olive or Grey Green)	45	20	10	10	15
Greywing (Skyblue, Cobalt, Mauve, Violet or Grey)	45	20	10	10	15
Cinnamon (Light, Dark, Olive or Grey Green)	45	20	10	10	15

REVISED SCALE OF POINTS **Remember: Condition is Supremely Important**	Size shape balance and deportment	Size and shape of head	Colour	Mask and spots	Wing markings
Cinnamon (Skyblue, Cobalt, Mauve, Violet or Grey)	45	20	10	10	15
Fallow (Light, Dark, Olive or Grey Green)	45	20	15	15	5
Fallow (Skyblue, Cobalt, Mauve, Violet or Grey)	45	20	15	15	5
Lutino	45	20	35	—	—
Albino	45	20	35	—	—
Opaline (Light, Dark, Olive or Grey Green)	40	20	†25	10	5
Opaline (Skyblue, Cobalt, Mauve, Violet or Grey)	40	20	†25	10	5
Opaline Cinnamon (Light, Dark, Olive or Grey Green)	40	20	†25	10	5
Opaline Cinnamon (Skyblue, Cobalt, Mauve, Violet or Grey)	40	20	†25	10	5
Opaline Greywing (Light, Dark, Olive or Grey Green)	40	20	†25	10	5
Opaline Greywing (Skyblue, Cobalt, Mauve, Violet or Grey)	40	20	†25	10	5
Yellow-faced (All varieties in Blue series except Pieds)	45	20	15	15	5
Pied (Dominant varieties)	45	20	§15	10	‡10
Pied (Clear Flighted varieties)	45	20	10	10	¶15
Pied (Recessive varieties)..	45	20	‡20	—	‡15
Dark-eyed Clear varieties	45	20	35	—	—
Lacewings	45	20	10	10	15

* Points allocated for depth of colour and clearness of wings.
† Including clear mantle and neck (10 points).
‡ Including contrast in variegation.
¶ Including clear flights and tail.
§ Includes band.
Teams of six birds of any one colour or teams of four birds of any one colour.
Points: General quality, 50; Uniformity, 50.

Interpretation of the Standard

The condition of an exhibition budgerigar is essential and if not in condition the bird cannot be considered for any award. Immediately we are faced, both as exhibitors and judges, with interpreting this. Is a bird with two flights missing or a spot absent necessarily out of condition? Does the appearance of a few undeveloped head feathers similarly bar a bird from winning any prize whatsoever? Any judge who rigidly applies the Standard and rejects completely on this sort of evidence is taking such a rule to extremes. Naturally such faults must push any exhibit further down in the awards, but where condition is concerned they should not be rejected at the outset. The basic interpretation of this rule is that a bird which is obviously in a bad moult, with a discoloured cere, lacking in tight feather or even ill at the time of judging is unfit for exhibition.

A great deal has been written on the subject of *type* and this word is used continually by all fanciers when describing the outline of a bird from below the neck. How the bird exhibits a straight backline with no apparent lump on the back of the neck, the wing tips just touching on the rump, the line beautifully continued right through to the tip of the tail is all important. Similarly the breast line should be full at the shoulder level, gradually sweeping through the feet with no looseness of feather under the rump and straight down to the tail. Any departures from these features and the bird is labelled as possessing 'poor type'.

A word on the long-flighted characteristics referred to in the Standard. Some years ago, principally in the 1950s, a large number of birds appeared with extra long tails and wings, resulting in hinged tail characteristics and the leading wing edge drooping well below the midline body areas. The number of primary feathers, instead of being seven was more often eight or nine. In addition, these birds had extra length of feather all over the head and body resulting in coarseness in the feather, but at the same time bigger heads and greater depth of mask. These latter desirable features tended to lead many judges to give them top awards until it was decided by the Budgerigar Society to ban, for the benefit of all concerned, any bird exhibiting long flights. This rule holds today, yet there are many champion breeders who say that every good stud has a long-flighted bird in evidence as a stock bird.

The head itself is vital in the exhibition bird and it is at the head qualities we look before any other feature when purchasing new stock. The immediate sweep up and away from the cere, gaining as much height as possible above the beak, is highly desirable. This must then round off in a smooth curve and, *without cutting away behind the eye,* must be maintained until the bird possesses a good depth of backskull before sweeping downwards. The frontal view is not depicted visually in the Ideal Budgerigar and one has to interpret the width of the head from the verbal description to begin with, until a certain amount of experience is obtained. Many beginners and novices imagine they have wide headed stock until they see the width on the champion birds. A great many birds in themselves show width and really appear to be wide across the eyes *but* they are small birds all round and in consequence fail when up against larger exhibits. The point you are looking for when examining width is a line immediately above the eyes when looking at the bird head on.

The eyes in a good example are hardly, if at all, visible from the front because of the rounded symmetry of the frontal skull. In addition the face has a flattish appearance from this angle, *the beak* being only just visible since it is tucked right into the face and mask. In profile it is essential that the beak does not protrude beyond a line from the front of the head to the chest. A glance at any pet bird will establish this point.

In a first-class exhibition bird the existence of a *neck* is difficult to determine since it has to be short and wide when looked at from any angle. The head effectively sits on the body and merges into it, any obvious neck being a fault.

The mask has to be clear, wide and – the point most difficult of all to maintain – as deep as possible. A close look at the Ideal reveals that there is a full $\frac{1}{2}$ in. between the beak and the base of the mask and, as established breeders will always tell you, the process of in-breeding tends each year to shorten this distance until eventually the spots appear immediately underneath the beak. Periodically therefore, a coarse feathered bird, possibly a long-flight, has to be used to keep the desired depth. Spots can either be too small or too large, though in the majority of cases they are too small. Breeders have difficulty in obtaining evenness of spot, the centre spots having a tendency to be slightly smaller than those nearer the cheek patches. In the past decade the opalines have maintained their spots extremely well, which has resulted in a boom in this variety and a regrettable decrease in others. However this situation is now rectifying itself. As to outsize spots, those at fault because they tend to touch or even overlap are easy to reduce in size by judicious breeding. Large spots draw attention to any unevenness in spacing. The Ideal depicts the six spots separated evenly across the mask; occasionally birds are seen with what is termed a 'bifurcated mask'. This simply means a split between the centre two spots up to the tip of the beak, resulting in a distinct division of the mask.

The remaining standards are self explanatory.

An additional point which is sometimes overlooked is character. You can possess the finest bird ever bred but if it is lacking in character

The Ideal
Budgerigar

The ideal length is 8½ inches from
the crown of the head to the
tip of the tail

then all is lost. Some birds have the ability to show themselves really well and because of their nature they sit calmly all day in the show cage, seemingly aware that they are being admired. Some, because they possess the correct features of width and depth of mask appear almost to be 'looking down their noses' and these qualities, coupled with the bird that has the big show temperament, is every fancier's aim.

The Budgerigar Society's Colour Standards

LIGHT GREEN
Mask, buttercup yellow, ornamented by six evenly spaced large round black throat spots, the outer two being partially covered at the base by cheek patches. Cheek patches: violet. General body colour: back, rump, breast, flanks and underparts, bright grass green of a solid and even shade throughout. Markings: on cheeks, back of head, neck and wings, black and well defined on a buttercup ground. Tail: long feathers, bluish black.

DARK GREEN
As above but with a dark laurel green body colour. Tail: long feathers, darker in proportion.

OLIVE GREEN
As above but with a deep olive green body colour. Tail: long feathers, darker in proportion.

GREY GREEN
The Grey Green conforms to the standard for Light Green except in the following details. Cheek patches: grey to slate. General body colour: dull mustard green. Tail: long feathers, black. (It should be noted that there are light, medium and dark shades of Grey Green.)

LIGHT YELLOW
Mask: buttercup yellow. Cheek patches: silvery white to very pale pinkish violet. General body colour: back, rump, breast, flanks and underparts, deep buttercup yellow and as free from green suffusion as possible. Primaries and tail: lighter than body. Eye: black pupil with white iris.

DARK YELLOW
Same as above but correspondingly deeper in colour.

OLIVE YELLOW
As above but with a mustard body colour.

GREY YELLOW

As above but with a dull mustard body colour. (It should be noted that there are light, medium and dark shades of Grey Yellow.)

SKYBLUE

Mask: clear white, ornamented by six evenly spaced large round black throat spots, the outer two being partially covered at the base by cheek patches. Cheek patches: violet. General body colour: back, rump, breast flanks and underparts, pure skyblue. Markings: on cheeks, back of head, neck and wings, black and well defined on a white ground. Tail: long feathers, bluish black.

COBALT

As above but with a deep rich cobalt blue body colour. Tail: long feathers, darker in proportion.

MAUVE

As above but with a purplish mauve body colour with a tendency to a pinkish tone. Tail: long feathers, darker in proportion.

VIOLET

As above but with a deep intense violet body colour. Tail: long feathers, darker in proportion.

GREY

Mask: white, ornamented by six evenly spaced large round black throat spots, the outer two being partially covered at the base by cheek patches. Cheek patches: grey-blue or slate. General body colour: back, rump, breast, flanks and underparts, solid grey. Markings: on cheeks, back of head, neck and wings, black and well defined on a white ground. Tail: long feathers, black. (It should be noted that there are light, medium and dark shades of Grey.)

WHITE

Mask: white. General body colour: back, rump, breast, flanks and underparts, white (suffused with the colour being masked). Wings and tail: white, bluish or light grey. (It should be noted that there are blue, cobalt, mauve, violet and grey shades in both light and dark suffusion.)

OPALINE LIGHT GREEN

Mask: buttercup yellow, extending over back of head and merging into general body colour at a point level with the butt of wings where undulations should cease thus leaving a clear V effect between top of wings so desirable in this variety, to be ornamented by six evenly spaced large round black throat spots, the outer two being partially covered at the base by cheek patches. Cheek patches: violet. General body colour: mantle (including V area or saddle), back, rump, breast, flanks and underparts, bright grass green. Wings: to be the same colour as body. Markings: should be normal with a suffused iridescent effect. Tail: long feathers, not to be lighter than mantle.

OPALINE DARK GREEN
As above but with a dark laurel green body colour. Tail: long feathers, not to be lighter than mantle.

OPALINE OLIVE GREEN
As above but with an olive green body colour. Tail: long feathers, not to be lighter than mantle.

OPALINE GREY GREEN
As above but with a dull mustard green body colour. Tail: long feathers, not to be lighter than mantle. Cheek patches: grey to slate. (It should be noted that there are light, medium and dark shades of Opaline Grey Green.)

OPALINE SKYBLUE
Mask: white, extending over back of head and merging into general body colour at a point level with the butt of wings where undulations should cease thus leaving a clear V effect between the top of wings so desirable in this variety, to be ornamented by six evenly spaced large round black throat spots, the outer two being partially covered at the base by cheek patches. Cheek patches: violet. General body colour: mantle (including V area or saddle), back, rump, breast, flanks and underparts, pure skyblue. Wings: to be the same colour as body. Markings: should be normal with a suffused iridescent effect. Tail: long feathers, not to be lighter than mantle.

OPALINE COBALT
As above but with a cobalt body colour. Tail: long feathers, not to be lighter than mantle.

OPALINE MAUVE
As above but with a mauve body colour. Tail: long feathers, not to be lighter than mantle.

OPALINE VIOLET
As above but with a deep intense violet body colour. Tail: long feathers, not to be lighter than mantle.

OPALINE GREY
As above but with a solid grey body colour. Cheek patches: grey to

slate. Tail: long feathers, no lighter than mantle. (It should be noted that there are light, medium and dark shades of Opaline Grey.)

OPALINE WHITE
As for White but with a suggestion of Opaline characteristics.

OPALINE YELLOW
As for Yellow but with a suggestion of Opaline characteristics.

OPALINE CINNAMON LIGHT GREEN
Mask: buttercup yellow, extending over back of head and merging into general body colour at a point level with butt of wings where undulations should cease, thus leaving a clear V effect between top of wings so desirable in this variety, to be ornamented by six evenly spaced large cinnamon brown throat spots; the outer two being partially covered at the base by cheek patches. Cheek patches: violet. General body colour: mantle (including V area or saddle), back, rump, breast, flanks and underparts, pale grass green. Wings to be same colour as body. Markings: should be normal cinnamon brown with a suffused opalescent effect. Tail: long feathers, not to be lighter than mantle.

OPALINE CINNAMON DARK GREEN
As above but with a light laurel green body colour. Tail: long feathers, not to be lighter than mantle.

OPALINE CINNAMON OLIVE GREEN
As above but with a light olive green body colour. Tail: long feathers, not to be lighter than mantle.

OPALINE CINNAMON GREY GREEN
As above but with a pale grey green body colour. Tail: long feathers, not to be lighter than mantle. Cheek patches: grey to slate. (It should be noted that there are light, medium and dark shades of Opaline Cinnamon Grey Green.)

OPALINE CINNAMON SKYBLUE
Mask: white, extending over back of head and merging into general body colour at a point level with butt of wings where undulations should cease, thus leaving a clear V effect between top of wings so desirable in this variety; to be ornamented by six evenly spaced large round cinnamon brown throat spots, the outer two being partially covered at the base by cheek patches. Cheek patches: violet. General body colour: mantle, back, rump, breast, flanks and underparts, pale skyblue. Markings: should be normal cinnamon brown on pale blue

ground with suffused opalescent effect. Tail: long feathers, not to be lighter than mantle.

OPALINE CINNAMON COBALT

As above but with pale cobalt body colour. Tail: long feathers, not to be lighter than mantle.

OPALINE CINNAMON MAUVE

As above but with pale mauve body colour. Tail: long feathers, not to be lighter than mantle.

OPALINE CINNAMON VIOLET

As above, but pale violet body colour. Tail: long feathers, not to be lighter than mantle.

OPALINE CINNAMON GREY

As above but with pale grey body colour. Cheek patches: grey to slate. Tail: long feathers, not to be lighter than mantle. (It should be noted that there are light, medium and dark shades of Opaline Cinnamon Grey.)

CINNAMON LIGHT GREEN

Mask: buttercup yellow, ornamented by six evenly spaced large round cinnamon brown throat spots, the outer two being partially covered at the base by cheek patches. Cheek patches: violet. General body colour: back, rump, breast, flanks and underparts grass green, 50 per cent or more of normal body colour. Markings: on cheeks, back of head, neck and wings, cinnamon brown on a yellow ground and distinct as in normal colour. Tail: long feathers, dark blue with brown quill.

CINNAMON DARK GREEN

As above but with a light laurel green body colour. Tail: long feathers, darker in proportion.

CINNAMON OLIVE GREEN

As above but with a light olive green body colour. Tail: long feathers, darker in proportion.

CINNAMON GREY GREEN

As above but with a pale grey green body colour. Cheek patches: grey to slate. Tail: long feathers, of a deep cinnamon shade. (It should be noted that there are light, medium and dark shades of Cinnamon Grey Green.)

CINNAMON SKYBLUE

Mask: white, ornamented by six evenly spaced large round cinnamon brown throat spots, the outer two being partially covered at the base by cheek patches. Cheek patches: violet. General body colour: back, rump, breast, flanks and underparts skyblue, 50 per cent or more of normal body colour. Markings: cheeks, back of head, neck and wings cinnamon brown on white ground and distinct as in normal colour. Tail: long feathers, blue with brown quill.

CINNAMON COBALT
As above but with pale cobalt body colour. Tail: long feathers, cobalt with cinnamon shade.

CINNAMON MAUVE
As above but with pale mauve body colour. Tail: long feathers, mauve with cinnamon shade.

CINNAMON VIOLET
As above but with pale violet body colour. Tail: long feathers, violet with cinnamon shade.

CINNAMON GREY
As above but with pale grey body colour. Cheek patches: pale grey. Tail: long feathers, pale grey with cinnamon shade. (It should be noted that there are light, medium and dark shades of Cinnamon Grey.)

GREYWING LIGHT GREEN
Mask: yellow, ornamented by six evenly spaced large round grey throat spots, the outer two being partially covered at the base by cheek patches. Cheek patches: pale violet. General body colour: back, rump, breast, flanks and underparts grass green, 50 per cent or more of normal body colour. Markings: on cheek, back of head, neck and wings should be light grey and distinct as in normal colour. Tail: long feathers, grey with pale bluish tinge.

GREYWING DARK GREEN
As above but with a light laurel green body colour. Tail: long feathers, darker in proportion.

GREYWING OLIVE GREEN
As above but with a light olive green body colour. Tail: long feathers, darker in proportion.

GREYWING GREY GREEN
As above but with a light mustard green body colour. Cheek patches: light grey. Tail: long feathers, dark grey. (It should be noted that there are light, medium and dark shades of Greywing Grey Green.)

GREYWING SKYBLUE

Mask: white, ornamented by six evenly spaced large round grey throat spots, the outer two being partially covered at the base by cheek patches. Cheek patches: light violet. General body colour: back, rump, breast, flanks and underparts skyblue, 50 per cent or more of normal body colour. Markings: on cheek, back of head, neck and wings should be light grey and distinct as in normal colour. Tail: long feathers, greyish blue tinge.

GREYWING COBALT

As above but with a pale cobalt body colour. Tail: long feathers, darker in proportion.

GREYWING MAUVE

As above but with a pale mauve body colour. Tail: long feathers, darker in proportion.

GREYWING VIOLET

As above but with a pale violet body colour. Tail: long feathers, darker in proportion.

GREYWING GREY

As above but with a pale grey body colour. Cheek patches: pale grey. Tail: long feathers, dark grey. (It should be noted that there are light, medium and dark shades of Greywing Grey.)

OPALINE GREYWING LIGHT GREEN

Mask: yellow, extending over back of head and merging into general body colour at a point level with butt of wings where undulations should cease, leaving a definite V effect between top of wings so desirable in this variety, to be ornamented by six evenly spaced large round grey throat spots, the outer two being partially covered at the base by cheek patches. Cheek patches: violet. General body colour: mantle (including V area or saddle), back, rump, breast, flanks and underparts, pale grass green. Wings same colour as body. Markings: should be normal and light grey in colour with suffused opalescent effect. Tail: long feathers, smoky grey.

OPALINE GREYWING DARK GREEN

As above but with a light laurel green body colour. Tail: long feathers, darker in proportion.

OPALINE GREYWING OLIVE GREEN

As above but with a light olive green body colour. Tail: long feathers, darker in proportion.

OPALINE GREYWING GREY GREEN

As above but with a light mustard body colour. Cheek patches: light grey. Tail: long feathers, dark grey. (It should be noted that there are light, medium and dark shades of Opaline Greywing Grey Green.)

OPALINE GREYWING SKYBLUE

Mask: white, extending over back of head and merging into general body colour at a point level with the butt of wings where undulations should cease, leaving a definite clear V effect between top of wings, so desirable in this variety, to be ornamented by six evenly spaced large round grey throat spots, the outer two being partially covered at the base by cheek patches. Cheek patches: violet. General body colour: mantle (including V area or saddle), back, rump, breast, flanks and underparts, pale skyblue. Wings same colour as body. Markings: should be normal and grey in colour with suffused opalescent effect. Tail: long feathers, grey.

OPALINE GREYWING COBALT

As above but with pale cobalt body colour. Tail: darker in proportion.

OPALINE GREYWING MAUVE

As above but with pale mauve body colour. Tail: darker in proportion.

OPALINE GREYWING VIOLET

As above but with pale violet body colour. Tail: darker in proportion.

OPALINE GREYWING GREY

As above but with pale grey body colour. Cheek patches: light grey. Tail: long feathers, grey. (It should be noted that there are light, medium and dark shades of Opaline Greywing Grey.)

YELLOW-WING LIGHT GREEN

Mask: buttercup yellow. Cheek patches: violet. General body colour: back, rump, breast, flanks and underparts, bright grass green. Wings: buttercup yellow, as free from markings as possible. Tail: long feathers, bluish. (*Note:* clearwings showing opaline characteristics should be shown in the A.O.C. or V class.)

YELLOW-WING DARK GREEN

As above but with dark laurel green body colour. Tail: long feathers, darker in proportion.

YELLOW-WING OLIVE GREEN

As above but with an olive green body colour. Tail: long feathers, darker in proportion.

YELLOW-WING GREY GREEN

This variety conforms to the standard of Yellow-wing Light Green except that general body colour should be dull mustard green. Cheek patches: grey to slate. Tail: long feathers, darker in proportion. (It should be noted that there are light, medium and dark shades of Yellow-wing Grey Green.)

WHITEWING SKYBLUE

Mask: white. Cheek patches: violet. General body colour: back, rump, breast, flanks and underparts, pure skyblue approximating to the normal variety. Wings: white, as free from markings as possible. Tail: long feathers, bluish. (*Note:* Clearwings showing opaline characteristics should be shown in the A.O.C. or V class.)

WHITEWING COBALT

As above but with a cobalt body colour. Tail: long feathers, darker in proportion.

WHITEWING MAUVE

As above but with a mauve body colour. Tail: long feathers, darker in proportion.

WHITEWING VIOLET

As above but with a violet body colour. Tail: long feathers, darker in proportion.

WHITEWING GREY

As above but with a grey body colour. Cheek patches: grey-blue. Tail: long feathers, grey. (It should be noted that there are light, medium and dark shades of Whitewing Grey.)

FALLOW LIGHT GREEN

Mask: yellow, ornamented by six evenly spaced large round brown throat spots, the outer two being partially covered at the base by cheek patches. Cheek patches: violet. General body colour: back, rump, breast, flanks and underparts, yellowish green. Markings: on cheeks, back of head, neck and wings, medium brown on a yellow ground. Eyes: red or plum. Tail: long feathers, bluish grey.

FALLOW DARK GREEN

As above but with a light laurel green body colour. Tail: long feathers, darker in proportion.

FALLOW OLIVE GREEN

As above but with a light mustard olive green body colour. Tail: long feathers, darker in proportion.

FALLOW GREY GREEN

As above but with a dull mustard green body colour. Cheek patches: grey to slate. Tail: long feathers, darker in proportion. (It should be noted that there are light, medium and dark shades of Fallow Grey Green.)

FALLOW SKYBLUE

Mask: white, ornamented by six evenly spaced large round brown throat spots, the outer two being partially covered at base by cheek patches. Cheek patches: violet. General body colour: back, rump, breast, flanks and underparts, pale skyblue. Markings: on cheeks, back of head, neck and wings, medium brown on a white ground. Eyes: red or plum. Tail: long feathers, bluish grey.

FALLOW COBALT

As above but with a warm cobalt body colour. Tail: long feathers, darker in proportion.

FALLOW MAUVE

As above but with a pale mauve body colour of a pinkish tone. Tail: long feathers, darker in proportion.

FALLOW VIOLET

As above but with a pale violet body colour. Tail: long feathers, darker in proportion.

FALLOW GREY

As above but with a pale grey body colour. Cheek patches: grey to slate. Tail: long feathers, darker in proportion. (It should be noted that there are light, medium and dark shades of Fallow Grey.) English and German forms are recognized: the German form having a white iris ring around the eye, the English form has none.

LUTINO

Buttercup yellow throughout. Eyes: clear red. Cheek patches: silvery white. Tail: long feathers and primaries yellowish white.

ALBINO

White throughout. Eyes: clear red.

YELLOW-FACE

All varieties in the blue series except Pieds. Mask: yellow only, otherwise exactly as corresponding normal variety. *Note:* yellow-marked feathers in tail permissible.

Pieds

DOMINANT PIED LIGHT GREEN

Mask: buttercup yellow of an even tone, ornamented by six evenly spaced and clearly defined large round black throat spots, the outer two being partially covered at the base by cheek patches. Cheek patches: violet. General body colour: as the normal Light Green variety but broken with irregular patches of clear buttercup yellow or with a clear yellow band approximately ½ in. wide round its middle just above the thighs. An all yellow or normal green coloured body should be penalized. Head patch is optional. (*Note:* all other things being equal, preference to be given, in accordance with the scale of show points, to birds showing the band.) Wings: colour and markings as the normal Light Green but having irregular patches of clear buttercup yellow or with part of the wing edges to shoulder butt clear yellow on an otherwise normal marked wing. Completely clear wings should be penalized. Wing markings may be grizzled in appearance. All visible flight feathers should be clear yellow but odd dark flight feathers are not faults. Tail: the two long tail feathers may be clear yellow, marked or normal blue-black in colour. Cere: similar to that of the normal Light Green or a mixture of normal colour and fleshy pink. Eyes: dark with light iris ring. Beak: normal horn colour. Feet and legs: blue mottled as the normal Light Green, fleshy pink or a mixture of both.

DOMINANT PIED DARK GREEN

As above but with general body colour as for normal Dark Green.

DOMINANT PIED OLIVE GREEN

As above but with general body colour as for normal Olive Green.

DOMINANT PIED GREY GREEN

As above but with general body colour as for normal Grey Green. Cheek patches: grey-blue to slate. (It should be noted that there are light, medium and dark shades of Dominant Pied Grey Green.)

DOMINANT PIED SKYBLUE

Mask: white, ornamented by six evenly spaced and clearly defined large round black throat spots, the outer two being partially covered at the base by cheek patches. Cheek patches: violet. General body colour: as the normal Skyblue variety but broken with irregular patches of white or with a clear white band approximately ½ in. wide round its middle just above the thighs. An all-white or normal blue coloured body should be penalized. Head-patch is optional (*Note:* all other things being equal, preference to be given, in accordance with the scale of show points, to birds showing the band.) Wings: colour and markings as the normal Skyblue but having irregular patches of clear white or with part of the wing edges to shoulder butt clear white on an otherwise normal marked wing. Completely clear wings should be penalized. Wing markings may be grizzled in appearance. All visible flight feathers should be clear white but odd dark feathers are not faults. Tail: the two long tail feathers may be clear white, marked or normal blue-black in colour. Cere: similar to that of normal Skyblue or a mixture of normal colour and fleshy pink. Eyes: dark with light iris ring. Beak: normal horn colour. Feet and legs: blue mottled as the normal Skyblue, fleshy pink or mixture of both.

DOMINANT PIED COBALT
As above but with general body colour as for normal Cobalt.

DOMINANT PIED MAUVE
As above but with general body colour as for normal Mauve.

DOMINANT PIED VIOLET
As above but with general body colour as for normal Violet.

DOMINANT PIED GREY
As above but with general body colour as for normal Grey. Cheek patches: grey-blue or slate. (It should be noted that there are light, medium and dark shades of Dominant Pied Grey.) *Note:* an Opaline, Yellow-face and Cinnamon form of Dominant Pied is recognized but these should only be shown in Dominant Pied classes.

CLEARFLIGHT LIGHT GREEN
Mask: buttercup yellow of an even colour ornamented by six evenly spaced clearly defined large round black throat spots, the outer two being partially covered at the base by the cheek patches. Cheek patches: violet. General body colour: as the normal Light Green with the exception of one small patch approximately $\frac{1}{2}$ in. by $\frac{5}{8}$ in. of clear buttercup yellow at the back of the head. Slight collar or extension of the bib, while undesirable, will not penalize. Wings: colour and markings as the normal Light Green but with seven visible flight feathers of clear yellow. Dark flights constitute a fault. Tail: the two long feathers should be clear yellow, dark tail feathers are a fault. Cere: similar to that of normal Light Green. Eyes: dark with light iris ring. Beak: normal horn colour. Feet and legs: blue mottled or flesh coloured.

CLEARFLIGHT DARK GREEN
As above but with general body colour as for normal Dark Green.

2

CLEARFLIGHT OLIVE GREEN

As above but with general body colour as for normal Olive Green.

CLEARFLIGHT GREY GREEN

As above but with general body colour as for normal Grey Green. Cheek patches: grey-blue or slate. (It should be noted that there are light, medium and dark shades of Pied (clear flighted) Grey Green.)

CLEARFLIGHT SKYBLUE

Mask: white, ornamented by six evenly spaced clearly defined large round black throat spots, the outer two being partially covered at the base by cheek patches. Cheek patches: violet. General body colour: as the normal Skyblue with the exception of one small patch approximately $\frac{1}{2}$ in. by $\frac{5}{8}$ in. of pure white at the back of the head. Slight collar or extension of bib, while undesirable, will not penalize. Wings: as normal Skyblue but with seven visible flight feathers of pure white. Dark flights constitute a fault. Tail: the two long feathers should be pure white, marked or dark tail feathers are a fault. Cere: similar to that of normal Skyblue. Eyes: dark with light iris ring. Beak: normal horn colour. Feet and legs: bluish mottled or flesh colour.

CLEARFLIGHT COBALT

As above but with general body as for normal Cobalt.

CLEARFLIGHT MAUVE

As above but with general body colour as for normal Mauve.

CLEARFLIGHT VIOLET

As above but with general body colour as for normal Violet.

CLEARFLIGHT GREY

As above but with general body colour as for normal Grey. Cheek patches: grey-blue to slate. (It should be noted that there are light, medium and dark shades of Clearflight Grey.) *Note:* An Opaline, Yellow-face and Cinnamon form of Clearflights is recognized but these should only be shown in Clearflight classes. The non-head-spot type of Clearflight (described as Australian) with full body colour is recognized and should be exhibited in Clearflight classes where these are provided.

DARK-EYED CLEAR YELLOW

Cheek patches: silvery-white. General body colour: pure yellow throughout and free from any odd green feathers or green suffusion. Wings: pure yellow throughout, free from black or grizzled tickings or green suffusion. All flight feathers paler yellow than rump colour. Tail: as the flight feathers. Cere: fleshy pink in colour as in Lutinos. Eyes: dark without any light iris rings. Beak: orange coloured. Feet and legs: fleshy pink. (*Note:* the actual body colour varies in depth according to the genetic makeup, i.e. whether light, dark or olive green, etc.)

DARK-EYED CLEAR WHITE

As above but with white body colour and free from any blue suffusion or odd blue feathers. Flights and tail: white. Cere: fleshy pink in colour as in Albinos. (*Note:* a dominant form is also recognized having normal cere, eyes, beak, feet and legs, which may be exhibited with the above-mentioned types of dark-eyed yellow and/or whites where separate classes are scheduled for this variety. A yellow-faced form of dark-eyed clear is also recognized but should only be shown in Dark-eyed Clear classes.)

RECESSIVE PIED LIGHT GREEN

Mask: buttercup yellow of an even tone. Throat spots: as the normal Light Green variety; may be present from one to full number. Cheek patches: violet, silvery-white or a mixture of both. General body colour: irregular patches of clear buttercup yellow and bright grass green with the latter mainly on the lower chest, rump and underparts. Zebra markings on the top of the head and around the eyes are not faults. Wings: black undulations or polka-dot markings should not cover more than fifteen to twenty per cent of total area. All visible flight feathers should be clear yellow but odd dark flight feathers are not faults. Cere: fleshy pink in colour as in Lutinos. Eyes: dark without any light iris ring. Beak: orange coloured. Feet and legs: fleshy pink.

RECESSIVE PIED DARK GREEN

As above with a yellow and dark green body colour.

RECESSIVE PIED OLIVE GREEN

As above but with a yellow and olive green body colour.

RECESSIVE PIED GREY GREEN

As above but with a yellow and grey-green body colour. Cheek patches: grey-blue or slate, or a mixture of both. (It should be noted that there are light, medium and dark shades of Recessive Pied Grey Green.)

RECESSIVE PIED SKYBLUE

Mask: white. Throat spots: as the normal Skyblue variety; may be present from one to full number. Cheek patches: violet, silvery-white or a mixture of both. General body colour: irregular patches of white and bright skyblue with the latter mainly on the lower chest, rump and underparts. Zebra markings on top of head and around the eyes are not faults. Wings: black undulations or polka-dot markings should not cover more than fifteen to twenty per cent of total area. All visible flight feathers should be white but odd dark flight feathers are not faults. Cere: fleshy pink in colour as in Albinos. Eyes: dark without any light iris ring. Beak: orange coloured. Feet and legs: fleshy pink.

RECESSIVE PIED COBALT
As above but with a white and cobalt body colour.

RECESSIVE PIED MAUVE
As above but with a white and mauve body colour.

RECESSIVE PIED VIOLET
As above but with a white and violet body colour.

RECESSIVE PIED GREY
As above but with a white and grey body colour. Cheek patches: grey-blue or slate, or a mixture of both. (It should be noted that there are light, medium and dark forms of Recessive Pied Grey.) *Note:* Opaline, Yellow-face and Cinnamon forms of Recessive Pied are recognized but these should be shown only in Recessive Pied classes.

LACEWING YELLOW
Mask: yellow, ornamented by six evenly spaced large round cinnamon throat spots, the outer two being partially covered at the base by cheek patches. Cheek patches: pale violet. General body colour: back, rump, breast, flanks and underparts, yellow. Markings: on cheeks, back of head, neck, mantle and wings, cinnamon brown on a yellow ground. Eyes: clear with light iris rings. Tail: long feathers, cinnamon brown. *Note:* the depth of yellow of the body colour, etc. varies according to the normal counterpart being masked by the Lacewing character, i.e. the richest yellow is carried by the Lacewing Olive Green and the lightest by the Lacewing Light Green.

LACEWING WHITE
Mask: white, ornamented by six evenly spaced large round cinnamon throat spots, the outer two being partially covered at the base by cheek patches. Cheek patches: pale violet. General body colour: back, rump, breast, flanks and underparts, white. Markings: on cheeks, back of head, neck, mantle and wings, cinnamon brown on a white ground. Eyes: clear red with light iris rings. Tail: long feathers, cinnamon brown. *Note:* the shade of white of the body colour, etc. varies only slightly in tone according to the normal counterpart being masked by the lacewing character. (A Yellow-faced form is recognized. Where no classes are scheduled for this variety it should be shown in any other colour classes.)

2. The Beginner

This chapter is directed at everyone who has never kept birds of any description and wishes to take up the challenge of breeding and exhibiting the beautiful budgerigar species.

First principles
Your first six months should be devoted to observing and considering all aspects of the hobby and making sure your money stays in the bank. Your first move should be to place an order with your newsagent for *Cage and Aviary Birds*, a weekly publication devoted to all varieties of caged birds. From this obtain the address of your area society and a local branch. Join your local club and you will soon learn from discussions at each meeting all sorts of detail that will help you understand a little better some of the difficulties that we all encounter.

Don't run away with the idea that breeding and exhibiting budgerigars is easy, even if you are successful as a beginner. When you climb up the ladder a little further you will soon find a bad season will occur and this will test your capabilities as a true budgerigar fancier. Obtain as many books as you can on the subject and perhaps, having decided by this time that you are the sort of person who can accept disappointments, visit one or two of the leading exhibitors. There is no substitute for seeing a top establishment first hand and obtaining ideas about the construction of your own aviary and how to feed your own stock.

Specialization
The range of colours available is very wide and were each of us to possess a wide group of these colours we would all have mediocre stock, unless of course money were no object. Nearly everyone specializes to some degree, the green series, including grey greens, being the most successful group in open competition. The skyblues are somewhat inferior in quality to the greens and grey greens and there are very few fanciers who have skyblues of super champion quality. To greens, or any other colour series for that matter, you may wish to add two sex-linked factors, opaline and cinnamon, either separately or together (see Chapter 8). Lutinos are very popular with some fanciers, but albino specialists are rare. The popularity of a colour series is generally related to those colours which are capable of winning 'Best in Show' awards.

Visit several shows before investing in stock and you should then be in a position to know the colour that particularly appeals to you. Act sensibly on the advice given and you could quickly be quite successful.

In conclusion, make sure you join the Budgerigar Society and your area society. The Budgerigar Society will allocate you a personal ring code, which you will keep for life. When the time comes for you to win your first red ticket, be modest and remember that your first placed bird in the beginner section probably will not even be considered in the novice section. Breeding exhibition budgerigars is an enormous challenge and success is not attained easily. If you can accept defeat quietly and learn from your mistakes, in time you will be a popular winner.

3. Aviaries

Newcomers to the hobby may have already started in an unambitious way in their shed in the back garden. Eventually the keen fancier will, depending on his financial position, want to improve his set-up, not only for his personal satisfaction but to improve his image with other fanciers. With the birds themselves and your show cages, your aviary is the third factor which contributes to your shop window.

Building regulations

Before contemplating any construction it is most important to consider local restrictions regarding the erection of buildings. For tenants of council owned property there are quite definite controlling clauses and to proceed blindly with building an aviary could cause unnecessary friction between tenant and council, resulting in the latter forcing the tenant to pull down the completed structure. A tactful approach, armed with a suitable set of drawings to show that you are not putting up a chicken run affair is far more likely to meet with a helpful attitude; however you must expect to be refused permission to lay down large concrete plinths in non-freehold property and there will be other regulations to which you will have to conform.

Owners of freehold property may still encounter great difficulties if they are not fully aware of the regulations appertaining to aviary construction. Some councils do not even know their own rules in this direction, yet others, happily in the majority, are fully conversant and prove extremely helpful. The correct procedure for a person who wishes to keep birds and erect an aviary for the purpose of pursuing his hobby, is that he does *not* have to have planning permission, but *must* comply fully with the local building regulations. There is a specific reference to the keeping of birds in the Town and Country Planning Act, which applies to the whole country and can be quoted when applying to any council. It applies only to freehold property of course and is as follows: 'Town and Country Planning Act, General Development Order 1963, Schedule 1, Part 1, Class 1, Section 2 . . . the keeping of birds does not require Planning Permission, as it is within the permitted use classes of the General Development Order, ancillary to the enjoyment of the dwelling house'. However, you must comply with the Building Regulations under Section 64 of the Public Health Act, 1936. You are breaking the law if you do not. For this you have to supply in addition to a set of the aviary plans in duplicate, two completed forms, a site plan and a

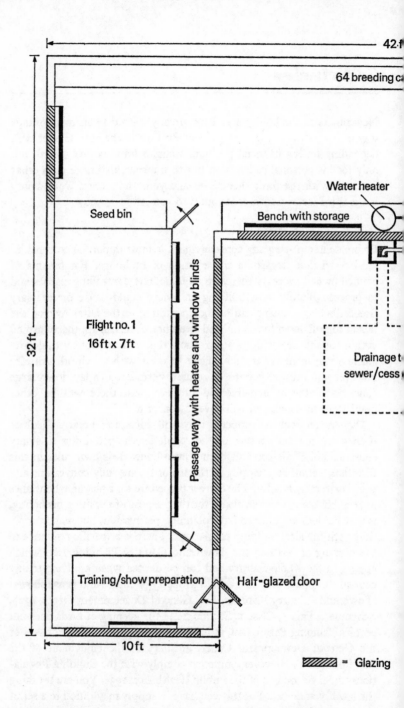

42·ft

64 breeding ca

Water heater

Seed bin

Bench with storage

Flight no. 1
16 ft x 7 ft

Passage way with heaters and window blinds

Drainage t
sewer/cess

32 ft

Training/show preparation

Half-glazed door

10 ft

▨ = Glazing

Plan for the author's aviary

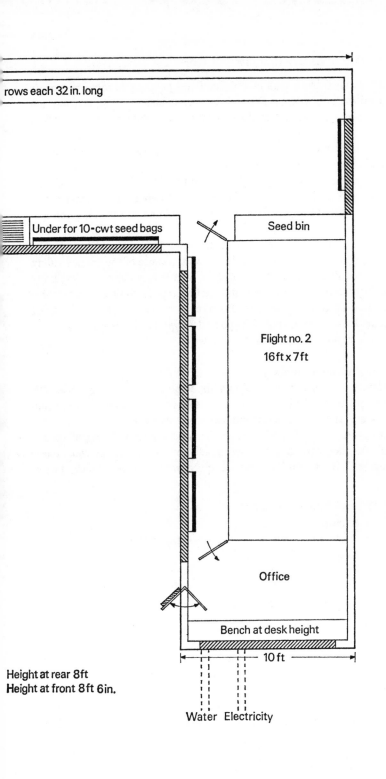

rows each 32 in. long

Under for 10-cwt seed bags

Seed bin

Flight no. 2
16 ft x 7 ft

Office

Bench at desk height

10 ft

Height at rear 8 ft
Height at front 8 ft 6 in.

Water   Electricity

more detailed block plan of your land and property in relation to your immediate neighbours. These are easily copied by tracing from the Ordnance Survey maps at the council offices, which are there for that purpose.

As an example, here are some of the conditions which applied to myself. I would have to have had a half hour fire resistant exterior on those sides bordering my neighbours' land, *if* I had the aviary right up to the land line. However I preferred a cedarwood exterior and therefore the area of the back and ends was calculated and then a given distance was stated for the birdroom to be *away* from the land lines (e.g. the rear face had to be 12ft. from the boundary). Also I had to have 5 in. by 2 in. cross beams in the roof because of the council ruling that I required fire resistant roof felts of two very heavy grades; lastly the birdroom had to have a half hour fireproof lining of a suitable material, such as Asbestolux. Hardboard is *not* acceptable. All these details have to be included in your description and it normally takes about a month for approval or otherwise.

Aviary requirements
Before embarking on any design for a new birdroom, consider the requirements of the budgerigars, your own comfort while attending your stock and the most efficient method of construction.

Budgerigars are happily one of the most accommodating of species and provided certain basic factors are not overlooked in your aviary they will thrive and reproduce quite satisfactorily. These factors are:

1 Avoidance of draughts.
2 Avoidance of damp.
3 Avoidance of sudden changes of temperature.
4 Avoidance of direct sunlight.
5 Adequate ventilation night and day.
6 A supply of artificial lighting as well as natural light.
7 Complete vermin proofing.

Heating is not in this list because while highly desirable in our climate, there are many aviaries throughout the country where heating has not been included, yet the birds in these establishments breed reasonably well. When it comes to your own comfort, however, there is nothing worse than embarking on a visit to your aviary under very cold conditions, knowing that by the time your chores are done you will be frozen to the bone. Artificial lighting is also a factor which contributes to your own comfort for without it you are helpless to give proper attention to your stock after dark.

STREAMLINING
One of the most annoying features of bird keeping is the continual circulation of moulted feathers, feather dust, excreta dust and so on, which easily accumulate in inaccessible places. If unsightly conditions are to be avoided, all your internal fitments must be streamlined and any dust traps boxed in or used as cupboards.

SIZE
From the time you enter the fancy as a raw beginner, right up to the time you are an open champion there is one fact which will irritate you continually. However big you build your aviary there comes a time when you wish you had built a bigger one. Forward planning is a must; always build in such a way that extensions can be added when necessary.

MATERIALS – BRICK OR WOOD?
One of my early avaries was constructed largely of brick and I had some of my finest seasons under its roof. Those of you who may have started breeding in your garage, adjacent to your house, may have experienced similar excellent results. This is due to the possible higher humidity level and greater control that a brick structure has in changing climatic conditions. In view of this I would say the ideal material for an aviary *is* brick. But to build an aviary using bricks adds enormously to the capital expenditure, so that the majority of us resort to the second choice of wooden cladded birdrooms. The use of timber does allow greater temperature changes, but by proper insulation, it is possible to control these.

My own aviary
My present birdroom incorporates the desirable features from all my previous rooms and excludes all the faults. This birdroom I will now describe at some length and from the illustrations of this aviary and other leading fancier's establishments it should be possible to construct any size of aviary along the correct lines.

When drawing the plans for my prospective birdroom I kept returning time and again to the basic plan of a magnificent birdroom built by William Watmough many years back at his home in Yorkshire. I felt that this aviary, with everything controlled from within, was the structure for me and I planned around this. It was also important to anticipate future enlargement of the structure as my finances at the time of building would not permit me to complete in one operation. I have progressed only as far as the basic rear birdroom to date and I intend to add two further wings. This first stage is 40 ft. by 10 ft. and to this I have recently added two temporary exterior flights to which I shall refer later.

The length of the aviary is of course dependent on the ground available but I have found from experience that a minimum width of 10 ft. is desirable for two reasons. First you will inevitably have fellow fanciers calling to see you and there is not sufficient room for a number of people in a narrower room. Second, you will be able to use outside nest boxes; a width of 10 ft. permits room for benching, people and protruding boxes and you will never regret the slight extra cost involved.

The feature I did not care for in the Watmough aviary was the internal flight along the front; I prefer internal flights at the extremities of my room. I also wished to control all windows from inside the birdroom rather than have the problem of closing windows from outside in bad weather.

CONCRETE BASE

The flat concrete base laid is 54 ft. by 16 ft. and on to this is laid a 39 ft. 9 in. by 9 ft. 9 in. by 1½ in. screed of fine grade concrete, ultimately to receive vinyl floor tiles. The main reason for the inclusion of the screed on top of the oversite at this early stage was so that the walls of the birdroom could sit on the edge of this raised area; rainwater then drains directly off to the surrounding pathway and cannot seep underneath and ultimately rot the framework.

FRAMEWORK AND EXTERIOR

The framework is of 4 in. by 2 in. sawn timber with 5 in. by 2 in. roof joists at 18 in. centres along the length of the birdroom. The walls are clad with ¾ in. shiplap cedarwood and the roof covered with ¾ in. plywood sheet. Two layers of bituminous felt, one grade 2B asbestos felt at 30 lb. and a top layer of 2C asbestos mineral finish felt are hot bonded to the roof plywood decking and finally covered with chippings. The finished roof is guaranteed for ten years.

WINDOWS

The eight windows are each 4 ft. by 3 ft. and include two lights, the uppermost opening outwards and hinged at the top to avoid direct rain entering the room. The lower light is fixed. Be careful not to have windows overlarge in your attempt to have as much natural light as possible entering the room. If you do, you may finish up with a greenhouse, with proportionally high summer temperatures, and budgerigars do not breed as well as they might in very bright surroundings. One of the well-known breeding partnerships in this country has made excellent use of plastic domed roof lights but, even with the installation of these superb looking and highly expensive items, they have occasionally found it necessary to whitewash the domes in order to reduce the heat that builds up quickly in hot weather.

VENTILATION

All birdrooms, whether large or small, must have adequate ventilation. Lack of ventilation in closed quarters may lead to the build up of disease in your stock. However it is important to avoid direct draughts on the roosting birds so in my own aviary I made three vents on the rear face of the birdroom, some 18 in. from the ground, and three corresponding vents high up on the front face. These are covered with zinc gauze and there is, as a result of this low/high positioning, a gentle flow of air at all times. I have also installed a fan extractor which is invaluable when cleaning out. During the day, in normal weather conditions, all windows are open from eight in the morning until six at night.

INTERIOR

To comply with the Building Regulations I was obliged to line the interior with a half hour fire resistant lining and I chose Asbestolux as the most reasonable lining. Because asbestos is poisonous it was vital that all joins were covered with quadrant or half-round beading in both flights in order to prevent the birds, particularly the hens, chewing this material. If the birdroom is lined in this way there is a resulting air gap between inner and outer shells and I strongly recommend this gap be filled with glass wool or other comparable insulating material. Glass wool is preferable because it prevents the access of rodents to the gap. The electrical wiring of course has to be installed prior to lining.

EXTERIOR

As a temporary measure I have constructed an outside flight at each end of the birdroom, each 10 ft. by 8 ft. I intend to dispense with these when the new wings are added. Each flight is constructed of 2 in. by 2 in. timber and is composed of four separate frames (i.e. three sides and a top) bolted together, the fourth side being the exterior wall of the birdroom. At one side is an entrance door sprung to close automatically behind me. This door is only 4 ft. high since all birds tend to fly high over your head whenever you enter a flight. There is the additional precaution of a small compartment inside the door so that I can enter one door, close it behind me and, having ensured there are no birds in the compartment, then enter the flight itself. All the flights are covered with heavy duty Twilweld wire mesh, double meshed to ensure complete safety for the birds from cats. Both exterior flights are covered with green translucent plastic sheeting to prevent any foreign matter such as poisonous leaves or excreta from infected wild birds dropping into the flight where it will be picked up by prize birds. All chewable surfaces and edges are protected; plastic edging is useful for this purpose. Each flight is raised on to a low brick wall and cemented into position and I have covered the concrete base with fine grade shingle. Any accumulation of excreta can be washed away by hosing through the drainage apertures in the brick walling.

The main aviary entrance door is placed centrally on the front face but has the added precaution of a safety door, also sprung, which closes automatically behind me as I enter. All opening windows have their own fixed safety screens on the interior face which allows full operation of the window, but prevents the escape of any stock which might have forced open a cage door.

The floor of my birdroom is covered with vinyl tiles which are simple to sweep and mop over and contribute to maintaining a high standard of hygiene.

ASPECT

A protected, southerly facing birdroom should be your aim. Avoid a north or easterly aspect if at all possible. There are many aviaries, particularly on the coast, where even with southerly aspects, as soon as the wind moves to the east the breeding results and hatchability of the eggs is markedly reduced.

4. Flights, Cages and Appliances

Interior flights
If possible there should be two window flights leading to outdoor flights; they should be at the extremities of your aviary so that the separated sexes continually call to one another, bringing both groups into breeding condition from time to time. You can manage with one flight but partnerships are then partially decided for you and difficulties may then arise when you choose your own pairings. On this basis, certain hens may refuse to accept the partners you choose—with poor if not negative results.

Interior flights are best constructed from 2 in. by 2 in. framing, with access doors about 4 ft. high.

Access to the outside flights
Some way for the birds to come and go to the outside flights has to be built and for the average-sized birdroom I would recommend a 10 in. square aperture. If it is larger heating control inside the birdroom becomes difficult, especially as breeding usually starts with most champions early in December. If it is smaller the birds may damage their wings on the frame and it is nearly always an important bird that hurts itself. When building these bob-holes, as they are usually known, do ensure that they are draught proof as far as possible when closed, as you will find that many birds will roost overnight alongside them, and if they get chilled will quickly succumb to pneumonia or enteric disorders.

Flight perches and feeding platforms
These are normally constructed of 2 in. by $\frac{3}{4}$ in. hardwood side supports, separated by $\frac{3}{4}$ in. dowel rods of the appropriate length, set at 8 in. centres. The completed perches are placed at 45 degrees in the flight so that birds on the higher perches do not excrete on those below. The diameter of the flight perches is important; when birds are caught up for show, they are unused to the smaller diameter show cage perches so they grip more tightly than normal and in doing so straighten up and improve their appearance.

Feeding trays and water pots should be raised from the floor of the flights on to a wide shelf or table. This should be clear of the perches in order to reduce contamination of the food and raised to assist those hens which for a variety of reasons put on weight or are simply very large show or breeding birds. I have lost many hens that have flown down at a steep angle to the feeding area on a concrete floor and become injured. This type of injury is often not apparent immediately and the bird may die some time later, the cause then being a complete mystery.

Painting and decorating

It is essential to use non-toxic leadless paints on all areas accessible to birds. Lead in any form is acutely poisonous and budgerigars continually chew any exposed surfaces. Painting the birdroom is an annual job, though the chore can be reduced, if you can afford it, by using laminated plastic wherever possible.

Seed bins/storage cupboards

Provision must be made for a number of seed bins containing the various types normally used. My own bins hold 3 cwt. in each compartment and have a chute to facilitate filling the mixing bowls which are in daily use. In addition you will require storage cupboards for items such as cuttlefish bone, millet sprays, grit, feeding pots, drinkers and so on. All the cupboards and bins in my own aviary have laminated tops which may be used as working surfaces.

Breeding cages

In all but a few expensive avaries, individual cages are provided to serve a number of purposes. Primarily their use is to provide a method of segregating breeding pairs of budgerigars in order to reproduce them on a controlled basis. They also have to act, at different times each season, as flight cages for young birds and for show teams. The cages may be required for sick birds if there is no alternative accommodation and lastly they have to house surplus stock when sales are being transacted.

These multi-purpose units can be easily constructed at home or bought from a recognized manufacturer but the minimum size for breeding quality stock is 24 in. long by 15 in. high and 15 in. deep. I prefer the height of each cage to be 18 in. for specific reasons which I shall refer to later. Every cage should be provided with a drawer type tray which can be taken out for regular cleaning.

The cage fronts are made from heavy gauge wire threaded through horizontal punched bars, preferably with a large swing door at least 7 in. square for easy access. If outside nest boxes are to be used, provision must be made for part of the top right hand section to be removable, enough for the 2 in. diameter nest box hole to be accessible to

1 *An ideal exterior nesting box.*

2 *Double drawer type nesting box as used by the author.*

3 *A perfect arrangement of interior flights.*

4 *A typical cage arrangement in a small aviary.*

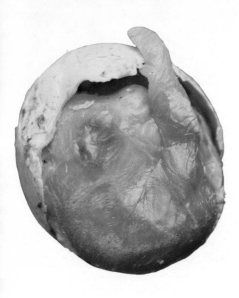

5 Dead-in-shell chick.

6 A freak caused by mutation, known as 'feather duster'. The bird is unlikely to live longer than 6 months.

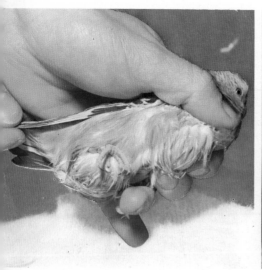

7 An egg bound hen unable to pass her first egg.

8 An example of the clear V or saddle required in opalines.

the breeding pair. All multi-purpose cages must be fitted with removable partitions to turn them into long cages and, if possible, the grooves where these slides fit should be made from aluminium, to prevent any chewing. The surrounds of the trays are also best protected with aluminium. All your cages should be provided with two ½ in. square hardwood perches which can be removed easily for cleaning. Square perches are essential for successful breeding since the round type become polished with use and when mating occurs the hen is unable to grip tightly when mounted, infertile eggs then resulting. Cages are best made from plywood, though a hardboard backing is acceptable, and leadless paints must of course be used to finish them. They should be sited facing the light, with the bottom row of cages raised at least 1 ft. from ground level, preferably on cage stands which can also serve as extra storage space.

Nest boxes

Every breeding pair has to be provided with some form of nest box which simulates the natural holes in trees used by the wild birds. Years ago it was accepted that most designs available on the market would satisfactorily answer the purpose but today top breeders, concerned with reducing egg and chick losses to a minimum, realize that the perfect design, correctly positioned, is vital.

The kind of nest box I now use is a drawer type design, which took some years to evolve, made from 8 mm. resin bonded plywood. At one period I used boxes which opened at one end by means of a top-hinged door; as one withdrew the concave base, which had no guarded sides, the door would sometimes drop down, smashing the eggs. A later improvement of this design had an inner box but this had only a 2 in. high surround to the removable concave, the result being that four week old chicks could jump over the back as one replaced the drawer, risking injury.

Today's design, which has given perfect results for many years, is an 8 in. by 6 in. by 7 in. high box. It has a 2¼ in. diameter entrance hole at one end, to accommodate the large show and breeding birds, and a hinged door at the other end. Within this box is a similar box, with a 2¼ in. hole lining up with the exterior aperture when the box is closed. At the opposite end of the inner box is a ¾ in. finger-hole. All four sides of the inner box, pinned directly to the concave, are 6 in. high. Ventilation holes are drilled through the longer sides of both boxes and a ⅝ in. square perch is provided under the entrance hole. The concave itself is at the opposite end. Operation is simple, tap the box gently to let

3

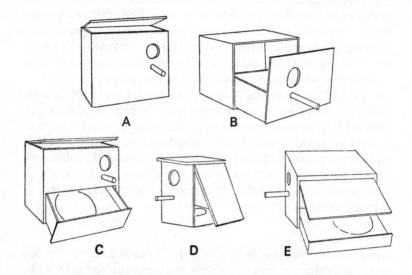

Design faults in nest boxes

A *This box is designed to be positioned inside the breeding cage, necessitating removal for inspection. If the hen has not left the nest she will be startled and may panic: damage to eggs or chicks by the disturbance is often considerable and the box may easily be dropped.*

B *This is a simple drawer-type box, but the drawer has to be gripped through the nest hole and if the parents have refused to leave they may cause damage by leaving over the sides of the box in a rush. Larger chicks tend to jump over the back of the inner box as it is being replaced after inspection, making it very easy to crush them.*

C *This box has all the disadvantages of (A). In addition, excreta and sawdust fall over the edges of the removable concave, which make it difficult to replace it. All the spilled material has to be cleaned each time from the main box. The spaces round the concave make it easy to damage the legs of the chicks.*

D *With this type of box eggs or chicks are almost certain to be dropped on to the cage floor.*

E *This type of box is better than those which are positioned inside the breeding cage and have to be completely removed for inspection, but the birds are still startled when the complete side wall is opened. When the concave has to be moved, eggs or chicks will easily drop off the unprotected sides.*

the occupants know you are about to inspect the inside; withdraw the inner box by means of the finger-hole and by this time the adult pair will have moved out quietly; then take the inner box to the bench for attention.

This design covers all eventualities. Nothing can get trapped at the sides of the concave or disturb the chicks and the eggs cannot roll away. The finger-hole prevents you dropping the box while carrying it to and from your bench and, since the complete box is bolted with 3/16 in. brass bolts to the top right hand corner of the breeding cage, no risks are entailed when visitors happen to brush against it. I used to be an advocate of boxes within the breeding cage but I found that placed with the entrance hole facing or partially facing the light, breeding results were moderate but not first class. However, if it is fixed on the front of the cage (hence the need for an 18 in. high breeding cage) with the hole facing away from the light, the hens enjoy the security of the near-dark interior of the nest box. I have found that the direct results are bigger clutches with perfect incubation; more eggs are hatched and feeding by the parents is improved. Lastly, with my type of double nest box and a heated birdroom, the thickness of the base concave is not so important as it might be in other circumstances. Nevertheless a full inch of wood from the base of the concave to the exterior is to be recommended. Do ensure that the concave is about 5 in. diameter and ½ in. deep and that no large flat areas exist around it where eggs or chicks can be pushed, with fatal results.

Some breeders prefer to use cardboard boxes placed on the floor of the cage. Others have upright boxes with lids which lift up exposing the whole scene, and there are many other variations. Nearly all have faults or drawbacks, so if you do decide to design your own model ensure all the factors I have mentioned are taken into account.

Water containers
The flights and the cages must be provided with fresh water every day. My flights are provided with half-pint containers consisting of a jam jar placed in a plastic receiver sold for this purpose. The filled receptacle can then be hung or placed on the feeding table in the appropriate flight. Water for the cages can be provided by plastic water founts which are fixed to the outside of each cage, the birds drinking the water from the 'finger' situated at the base of the fount. These founts are referred to as Flomatic Founts and are easily obtainable. The disadvantage of these founts lies in the fact that if you have many they are time consuming to clean each day, so I now use 3 in. by 1½ in. pottery

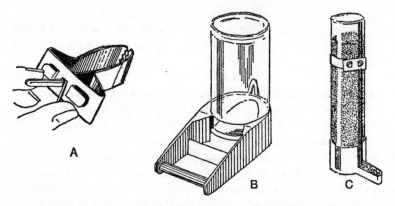

A

B

C

A *A cuttle-fish holder: this is fixed to the bars of each breeding cage, on the inside.*

B *A water fount suitable for the flights: it is an inverted jam-jar on a formed plastic base.*

c *A Flo-matic Feeder. This is ideal for seed and water in the breeding cages.*

vessels placed on the floor of each cage. Both types become fouled each day, necessitating cleaning; it is a matter of preference which you use.

Seed hoppers/trays

Automatic hoppers are frequently used in aviaries. The hopper contains perhaps 14 lb. seed and as the seed is consumed at the base the uneaten grain slides down from above. In practice, the seed husks and very fine dust which accumulate block up the feeding area and the birds, though they may not starve, do not get sufficient food at all times and growth is impeded. I prefer to use enamel dishes in the flight and two or three smaller dishes in each of the breeding cages. One is necessary for the staple mixture, another for soaked grain and a third for any supplementary mixtures you may give whilst breeding is in progress. The expense of enamel dishes will be well repaid as they last for years. One word of advice – do ensure the dishes, if coloured, are not red since this colour always upsets budgerigars to an alarming degree.

5. Buying Stock

After some months of study of what is required for exhibition, and having built your aviary, you will now be anxious to stock it properly. Naturally you want as many birds as possible of the intended specialized colour and assuming you have built an average sized aviary, with twelve breeding cages, you would like to make full use of them. The chances are that you are running low on finance by the time you've reached the stock purchasing stage, but *still* the idea of filling all the cages will persist. Resist that temptation, for it is vital that you purchase the minimum number of birds required for a successful start, of the best quality that you can afford.

The next question is whom to approach for the stock. You should have widened your appraisal of the exhibition world beyond your local societies during the waiting period. Remember that it will be at these local societies you first exhibit and that you will be aiming to beat the other exhibitors. To buy from them is therefore probably not advisable. Even as a beginner, if you purchase the right material from outside your area there is a good chance you can breed birds capable of beating the local champions. You now are going further afield, perhaps twenty to a hundred miles away. The distance doesn't matter; what does matter is that you buy the sort of bird that suits you from a successful breeder and exhibitor of your choice. Even as a beginner, you should preferably buy from a champion exhibitor known to be breeding quality youngsters every season. Beware of buying from the best in show winner who has won with a bought bird and has little to back it up in the way of current year stock. Choose a champion whose top priced birds are well beyond your means and buy of his less expensive stock – it will still be good. By concentrating not only your initial spending on this successful man but your future requirements for years to come, you will have the advantage of continually breeding with related stock. This way you will have far greater potential to produce winners than the purchaser who buys from a dozen different sources. You can slowly increase your quality each season by buying a more expensive bird each time, knowing that your breeding is successful and that your team is already being noticed on the showbench. Apart from perhaps one outcross in five years time you should be able to stay with this champion for some considerable time, assuming you chose correctly in the first place and he is still winning at his level.

How much to spend

There are certain rules to obey when buying as a beginner. To pay too little (by which I mean pet-shop prices) is unwise since you will realise eventually that the quality of the birds offends you and it will have been money wasted. I generally advise newcomers to spend between £5 and £10 per bird depending on their resources. I would further qualify this recommendation by saying that even if you can afford it, don't invest more because there is so much you have to learn in the first five years. Birds in this range are of good quality, well worth building on for the future and have a good resale value provided that they are not too old.

The beginner, and indeed many more experienced fanciers, are puzzled by how a bird is priced. Some of the leading fanciers in the hobby price their stock on relationships to winners or on the fact that the bird has won a first at an Open Show. Should the show be the Budgerigar Society Club Show or the National Show then the price will be that much higher. Others prefer to price on more tangible factors that both the buyer and the seller can see in the form of quality. When I am selling I take into account every feature the bird possesses or lacks and arrive at a reasonable, acceptable figure. I am not concerned with the fact that a bird may or may not be the sister to a second National winner. It has some bearing, of course, but it is the visual features I am most concerned with. Two first National winners will not necessarily breed any more winners since livestock never behaves like a machine. The price you pay should be related largely to the qualities of the head, and perhaps the colour if it is, for example, a lutino.

Quantity

Working on the twelve breeder sized establishment, buy in June of any year six hens and four cocks all known to be proven as breeders and all aged between fifteen and twenty months. This time of year is best because nearly all breeders have completed their results by May and their adult breeding stock is consequently in reasonable condition in June to be sorted for sale. The excess of hens over cocks is recommended because invariably the hens cause trouble in one way or another and it is unlikely that, with just four pairs, all eight birds will be in breeding condition at one time. This imbalance in numbers solves many of the problems. Proven breeders are preferable for the beginner since he will have enough problems without worrying about untried stock in his first year. The ages mentioned are right for you to expect the birds to give of their best to their new owner.

Purchasing for an established stud

Whether a novice or a champion, you must take stock each season of the main failing in your stud. If you decide that all your birds are short in mask or lacking in backskull, go out and buy a cock bird to counteract the fault. It is no use simply buying a good bird every year thinking that your problems will be overcome this way. He must have some specific point which will improve your existing stock. Think carefully and act sensibly and your money will be wisely spent.

Points to consider while purchasing

There are a series of points which every intending purchaser should check once he has decided that a particular bird is exactly what he wants.

1 Are the droppings normal or not?
2 Are the irises of the eye white or bloodshot?
3 Has the bird a hunched, liverish look?
4 Are the feathers, particularly the flights, curved at the tips, denoting nervous habits?
5 Is the bird in good condition; if so, is it vigorous and alert or is it a lethargic, quiet type needing a very compliant partner?
6 Is the bird full to the touch, without a sharp breastbone?
7 Is there any sign of lumps or cysts, especially round the vent?
8 Is the breeder feeding the bird in the same way that you will, or is he giving it something special, the absence of which will adversely affect your purchase?
9 If the bird has bred, is the breeding record card forthcoming?
10 What is the bird's reaction to the opposite sex? If the breeder doesn't object, this is always a good guide.

Satisfied on these matters, ask yourself once again if you really like the bird or if you are wavering. Adopt the policy of 'when in doubt don't' invest. It has been said that you become a real fancier only when you can travel several hundred miles to another stud with as much money as you need and still go home with your money because you are not happy with what you have seen.

The Winning Stud

A stud in the true sense is a collection of high quality livestock, each kind having a related likeness to one another and as a group distinguishable to a certain owner. Any departure from this and all you have is a collection of birds. The object of us all is to establish a winning strain, however small, of high class budgerigars so that any member of the fancy can say 'that's one of so-and-so's birds', without having to check in the catalogue first. Of course, if the stud has a basic fault throughout this is a disadvantage since this immediately penalises the stud for an indefinite period. The only correct way of breeding a winning stud is to mate relatives to one another in order to consolidate the best points, at the same time attempting to banish the faults.

It is not necessary to be the owner of a large stud to have a team of birds which are highly sought after by other members of the fancy. There are countless examples of breeders who have 'clicked' with pairing their birds over a few seasons and who subsequently are chased to part with the excellent progeny produced. Unfortunately big offers are very tempting and perhaps the breeder feels 'well I've still got the parents so the youngsters may as well go'. He sells and the youngsters are spread around where they soon lose their individual identities with other breeders and the beginnings of a true stud are lost. The founding of a strain takes considerable patience over a number of years. If the time spent in establishing that strain were to be translated into terms of actual cash, offers to buy might not then be so attractive. These studs take years of hard work and when one takes into account that every fancier has to develop his 'eye' in the beginning to know exactly what is required on the showbench, then selling all you have strived for seems foolish.

Aiming for quality
All serious breeders place the quality of their birds before anything else. Each season, around September time, inspect every bird in the aviary and rigorously cull out those which fall below a certain standard, the aim being to raise that minimum standard each year. I wasted several seasons many years ago by retaining certain borderline stock which I knew had been produced by my better lines, when, with hindsight, it is now obvious they should have been sold. Pedigree is important but it should take second place to appearance. If a bird does not have the right visual quality, then irrespective of its parentage, it must be rejected.

Advance planning
Every season when pairing up your stock, plan at least two seasons ahead and envisage the building or continuation of the best lines. You may for example, having purchased a superb cock bird, decide that it is necessary to bring his qualities to bear as quickly as possible and therefore you choose four desirable hens to pair him with in that season. Immediately you should be planning ahead, assuming that each pairing

will be successful, and calculating the line breeding and possible in-breeding pairings for the following years. Just to pair such a cock to one hen for two rounds is not good enough in the established stud. Such a bird has to be made available to a number of lines if he was worth buying in the first place. When planning ahead for a whole stud of perhaps two hundred birds, life can become very complicated but in practice one is concentrating these plans on the very best lines in the stud. The pairing of relatives is discussed fully in Chapter 7.

Speculate to accumulate
I have always been a firm believer in speculating on at least one outcross cock every year if the right bird is obtainable. To sit back and withdraw the proceeds of your sales from the stud completely in any season is unwise. There is always one line in the stud that could do with improvement. There is little point on the other hand in buying a range of outcrosses which will confuse your long-term plans. Far better to choose one or two superb cocks, even if they cost you the whole of the season's proceeds. They will give you far more satisfaction because they should be better than anything else you possess and your aim must be to bring the stud up to their higher qualities. Having effected this improvement over two or three seasons, the quality of your surplus stock also improves and thereby you accumulate greater rewards from sales.

When things go wrong
You may as well accept that at some time in your livestock career you will run into trouble and produce in a whole season only a few birds of mediocre quality. If you run into this sort of season you can be certain that the fault lies with your management. It could be neglect on your part, or perhaps over enthusiasm to the extent that you have overdone the vitamins. Whatever the trouble happens to be, sit down, analyse the season with particular attention to any structural or feeding alterations, and there will be a reason there somewhere. It is a wise practice to note, while you are successfully producing winners, every item that is being fed, the quantity that is being given, the amount of daylight and artificial light and so on. Should matters subsequently turn sour you can refer back and check for changes.

Selection of breeding stock
To ensure a reasonable chance of success in any season always make sure that the proportion of hens to cocks is approaching two to one by

the time pairing takes place. At this time my birdroom has sixty cocks and just over a hundred hens, with forty two breeding cages in use. This allows for inevitable losses in the breeding pens, the odd bird succumbing to disease or found dead in the flight and so on. In addition there are always problems such as egg binding, refusal to lay perhaps due to immaturity, hens that chew their eggs and so on. Do not make the mistake of selling down to the barest number of set pairs. No stud of any consequence has had a trouble-free season yet.

The attention given to the hens is of paramount importance. One can always purchase a good cock but to obtain a hen of equal calibre is nearly always difficult. To pair a greatly inferior hen or hens to a good cock is stupid, so it is important to retain a high percentage of really desirable hens for your personal use each season. A feature I like to see in breeding hens more than any other is great thickness across the area which would normally be termed the back of the neck. Those with this feature, which also means that there will be no appearance of shoulder, generally have good backskull as well, though the two areas are not to be confused.

With these points in mind the beginner or novice would be well advised to obtain the services of a more experienced fancier when deciding on which birds to retain and which to sell. The fact that a second opinion is available at such a time is always welcome, since when dealing with a large number of birds at one time you tend to overlook certain features that you would normally notice under quieter circumstances. The fancier and the adviser should decide beforehand that they will be quite ruthless in their assessments and discard any bird not reaching the standard required. Every bird should be caged individually and each feature judged. All birds of the same sex and colour group, for example all the green cocks, should be assessed together looking at their visual qualities first. Some are obvious 'not for sale' birds and similarly others definitely have to go. The few in the middle must be noted carefully and I tend at this stage to keep the first borderline bird back to allow for any future mishaps. Do not, while assessing, become head or spot conscious to the extent that you ignore type with the result that the following season you have a large proportion of big headed birds all with hinged tails. The best all round birds must be retained. Having done one section move on to the next and so on until every bird has been severely criticized. Should, in the opinion of the adviser, the birds as a whole be completely wrong, then it is his duty to voice his opinion to that effect so that the breeder can alter his complete approach over the next few seasons.

Selecting the pairs – outcrossing

The first step for the newcomer is almost certainly to mate the best cock to the best hen, assuming the two birds are not an unsuitable colour pairing. If he adopts this policy throughout, ignoring colour by and large and concentrating on the show points, then results should be satisfactory. Never mate two birds when both have the same fault. Beginners and novices obviously have far more headaches to resolve than does a champion in this respect. The system of best to best will probably continue for quite a few seasons until the breeder realizes he is winning on the show bench and is making progress. Having reached this stage, then and not before is the time to consider the possibilities of mating relations which is referred to as line breeding or inbreeding. These practices can, if successful, really put the breeder on the map and give a degree of uniformity throughout his stud. So concentrate for a few years on the complete elimination of undesirable faults and this should provide the initial stock on which to fix the standard of excellence we all desire.

Yellows and Buffs

I. YELLOW. Although an adjective describing a colour this does not apply exclusively to colour when talking about budgerigars. It refers to a bird of small to average size, with short, fine quality feathering, with distinct wing markings and a high grade sheen when the bird is in condition. The breast is of even colour and the colour is sharp and lustrous. Head qualities are poor to average, as indeed are spots.

2. BUFF. By contrast, the term buff is applied to a bird of greater size than average, coupled with loose, coarse feathering which if examined proves to be of greater length than normal. The head and spots are much greater in size than normal, though usually poorly shaped, and the tail and flights are also excessively long. Markings are not clearly defined and in general such birds exhibit poor type.

Every stud should possess a percentage of buffs and yellows. The majority of establishments comprise solely yellows with the result their birds never progress beyond a certain size, although the colours are good. This is also one of the basic reasons the novice visitor to the champion establishment expresses surprise at the size and quality he sees, which is not entirely the result of expert feeding.

There are basic rules to adopt when pairing, assuming a percentage of clearly defined buffs are available.

1 Breeding 'buff to buff' will perpetuate large, rough feathered, unshapely stock useless for exhibition.

2 Breeding 'yellow to yellow' will perpetuate small bodied birds, lacking in depth of mask and spots.

3 Breeding periodically 'buffs to yellows' will introduce the coarser features to the finer features with the aim of reproducing big, well shaped birds with ample width, depth of mask and symmetrical spots, yet also having type and fineness of feather.

Obviously there are many birds, especially those obtained as outcrosses, which are impossible to define as either buffs or yellows. It does not necessarily follow that they are good specimens all round. Only the skilful breeder, who knows his stock thoroughly and takes full note of all birds with buff or yellow backgrounds, can hope to apply this theory to full advantage.

6. Feeding

The Digestive System

The human digestive system is referred to as the alimentary canal and in birds likewise, but in birds it is shorter and modified to suit the species. The system starts with the beak, which in the budgerigar consists of a strong lower mandible overlapped by a formidable upper mandible which is the feature associated with all parrot-like species. The purpose of the beak in this seedeater, is to dehusk and crush seeds of all descriptions prior to swallowing them.

Throat and crop

The process of swallowing in the budgerigar is achieved by the pharynx and larynx, which ensure the food is directed down the gullet. There it is mixed with saliva before being deposited in a bag-like organ, the crop, where it remains temporarily and is softened, but not digested. The crop walls have the remarkable function of producing crop 'milk', which is a cellular mixture containing fat and protein. From the moment of mating, the external layer of cells within the crop which produce the milk increase their rate of division by 600 per cent. The milk is a source of great interest to breeders who wonder why a newly hatched chick can double its weight in a matter of hours and continue this enormous rate of growth over a few weeks. Crop milk is rich in vitamins, particularly vitamin A and all of the B group. The chemistry of crop milk is not fully understood but it is believed by many that poor quality crop milk in budgerigars is likely to result in a high incidence of French moult (page 168.)

The gizzard and grit

The first part of the 'stomach' is called the proventriculus; this leads directly to the second part, the gizzard. The gizzard is a strong organ composed of thick walled muscle which undergoes several contractions every minute. The budgerigar selects and swallows suitable grit, which is retained while still sharp edged within the gizzard; this grit grinds and separates the food as it passes through the gizzard. Grit falls into two groups, insoluble grit, mainly in the form of quartz, and soluble grit from the limestone group. The latter tends to dissolve readily and be passed through after a while, but the breeder must ensure that both types of grit are offered since the limestone, in the process of dissolving, provides essential calcium to the body. Regular replenishment of the grit trays is vital since budgerigars are very selective and will not make use of very fine particles, prefering the larger coarse grains found in most proprietary mineralized grits.

The intestines

The intestine is divided into two parts, the small and large intestine. The former is basically concerned with the absorption of nutritious material into the bloodstream while the latter deals with the excretion of the waste products via the cloaca. The first section of the small intestine is the duodenum, into which two ducts empty their contents. One duct secretes bile from the liver, which dissolves the fats, and the other duct is from the pancreas, which exudes starch reducing fluids on to the food passing through the intestine.

The liver

This is the largest organ in the body and has approximately forty functions. Many of its functions are concerned with digestion, but other important functions include the destroying of bacteria and the conversion of excess ammonia from protein metabolism into urea (metabolism is the burning of food and its utilization by the body). The liver is also a storage reservoir of food for energy in the form of blood sugar.

Excretion

The large intestine is responsible for the excretion of the waste products but the kidneys also contribute to this end. The function of the kidneys is to act as filtration organs for the blood system, removing the urine and passing it down the ureter into the cloaca. While in the cloaca, the urine loses water rapidly and becomes a concentrated white precipitate of uric acid, which is the white portion found in bird droppings.

The Chemistry of Foods and Feeding

There is little doubt that knowledge of this subject means the difference between success or failure in breeding budgerigars. There are a vast number of ex-fanciers who have fallen by the wayside as a direct result of disappointments in the breeding room, basically caused by lack of attention to the dietary requirements of their stock. There is an old phrase often repeated amongst breeders of any livestock, 'you only get out what you put in', this is true of budgerigars as of any other animal or bird.

Budgerigars are unquestionably vegetarian. Their main natural food is grain, plus added plant material. However, in the wild, insects have often been found in the crops, so it is obvious the birds will digest animal protein willingly and any fancier will tell you that a spider found in the aviary flight is quickly attacked and consumed. It is obvious from this that in some way we have to supplement the basic grain and water diet if we are to be at all successful breeding show quality specimens, it must also be remembered that we are raising stock under entirely artificial conditions and that *we* are the only providers when it comes to food.

The study of nutritional science has, since the turn of the century, occupied many laboratories throughout the world and yet for all our up to date knowledge there are few of us who apply it to our birds.

Suppose we therefore correct ourselves and study the foods budgerigars eat, the elements of which they are composed and how every bird breaks them down from the moment of swallowing. Foods are composed for the main part of carbohydrates, proteins, fats, mineral salts, vitamins and water.

Carbohydrates

These are chemical compounds which are synthesized by plants to store their own supplies of fuel. There are three kinds of carbohydrate, each having slightly different but related functions.

(a) Sugars – to provide energy quickly.
(b) Starches – to provide energy slowly.
(c) Cellulose – to provide, for plants, a structural supporting framework of cells.

Sugars – glucose/fructose/sucrose

In composition, glucose is one of the simple sugars and one of the first sugars produced in leaves. The sweet taste at the base of a grass stalk is glucose. It occurs in the blood of animals and is the form in which fuel or energy is transported within the body. It becomes converted into fructose, another similar sugar, during the process of the release of energy. Sucrose or common sugar is a combination of glucose and fructose, and in addition to more commonplace sources, occurs naturally in roots such as carrots. Sugars are essential to life since, with any sudden surge of body actions, it is the sugars which provide that energy very quickly when called upon.

Starch

A grain of seed consists of a small dormant embryo. This is in reality the germ from which the new plant would develop if planted and watered. It is separated from the larger part of the seed grain by a plate of tissue called the scutellum, but of course it is the larger part which is the food store for the early growing period of the plant. This stored food, protected by outer husk, is composed of granules of starch. Starch granules are designed to preserve the starch during the time the various cereal grains are dormant, and as such are resistant to digestion. It is for this reason the bird grinds the grain up, so that the body heat can swell the granules which burst, and the starch is then in a digestible form.

Proteins

Proteins are composed of carbon and hydrogen which are combusted to yield energy for the body; in addition there are units called amino acids and it is this group of acids which in turn produce nitrogen. Protein is the real material of all living bodies of plants and animals and is vital for growth. It is essential for the function of reproduction and for combating injury or disease, when damaged body tissues have to be replaced.

There are two sources of protein in nutrition, those from animals and those from plants. Animal proteins are derived from meat, fish, eggs, milk and milk products such as dried milk, evaporated milk and cheese. Vegetable proteins are derived from cereal grains, nuts (in particular peanuts), green leafy plants, peas, beans and root vegetables to a minor extent. Protein eaten as food is digested into its component amino acids. There can be more than twenty different kinds of amino acids in a particular protein and perhaps a gross total of many hundred amino acid units in all. The digestion of a growing bird disconnects all these amino acids from the different articles in the diet and rearranges them in the correct proportion to construct his own bird protein. Of the more than twenty different kinds of amino acids, the body can manufacture certain specific ones. However there are about ten amino acids that it cannot produce, which must be added by diet. These ten amino acids are contained in the animal and vegetable protein groups referred to earlier, but one group on its own is insufficient to cover all ten absent items. If derived from, say, just vegetable sources such as seed grains and bread, the body can never complete the building up of protein. For this reason vegetable proteins are referred to as 'second class' proteins. Animal sources on the other hand are more complete and a diet containing meat, milk and eggs would provide a greater proportion of the essential amino acid group. It is therefore obvious that a budgerigar, being a vegetarian, has to have a supplementary source of animal protein, if perfect health and reproduction are to be anticipated. Remember – the animal proteins are referred to by nutritionists as 'first class' proteins.

Not all budgerigar fanciers stop to appreciate fully the growth rate from the moment of hatching to the moment of first arriving on the perch; this is so rapid that it is hardly credible. In order to assist this rapid growth rate in the pedigree budgerigar, it has been estimated that the amount of complete protein required has to be in the region of 20 per cent. A purely grain diet would only contain in the region of 15 per cent and would undoubtedly rear most chicks satisfactorily, but not the big framed exhibition youngsters; these demand a much higher proportion of protein to avoid such food deficiency setbacks as French moult (see page 168). In America research on growing poultry chicks recommends that fast growing breeds need at least 7 per cent more protein than the others and this has to be administered to the adults for their crop milk which in turn is fed to the young chicks. It is also stated that crop milk should contain 58 per cent protein and that the protein must be of a high quality, containing both animal and vegetable proteins. (Feathers are very high in protein.)

TABLE I

AMINO ACIDS

Essential requirements for growing chicks	Per cent of diet
Tryptophan	1·1
Lysine	2·4
Phenylalanine	1·3
Leucine	1·4
Valine	0·8
Isoleucine	0·72
Methionine	0·7
Histidine	0·15
Threonine	0·6
Arginine	1·2

TABLE II

AMINO ACIDS IN CERTAIN FOOD ITEMS

	Tryptophan	Lysine	Phenylalanine	Leucine	Valine	Isoleucine	Methionine	Histidine	Threonine	Arginine
Millet	1·9	3·7	4·5	9·3	6·2	5·9	1·9	1·6	—	—
Oats	1·3	3·4	4·8	5·7	6·6	5·1	1·5	1·5	3·4	6·7
Wheat Germ	2·9	5·1	4·1	6·6	6·3	3·8	2·8	4·3	3·0	9·6
Cabbage	0·9	3·9	1·9	3·7	4·0	3·1	1·3	2·1	2·8	7·3
Meat	0·6	6·1	5·1	8·0	6·1	1·4	1·1	3·4	5·5	5·4
Milk (whole)	1·1	8·4	5·3	10·1	6·7	6·5	2·1	2·8	4·8	3·6
Milk (dry skimmed)	1·5	8·7	4·5	10·9	5·9	5·1	2·2	2·5	4·7	—

TABLE III

THE FAT CONTENT OF CERTAIN FOODS
(g. per oz.)

Milk	1·0
Milk (condensed)	2·6
Eggs	3·3
Wholemeal bread	0·6
Oats	2·5
White bread	0·2
All fruits	Nil
Greenfoods	Nil

Fats

Of all the components of a diet, fat is the most concentrated source of energy. Although starch is the common energy-storage substance in cereal grains, some plants have the ability to store energy in the even more compact form of fat. When linseed, for example, ripens, the amount of starch falls and the fat rises, and oil seeds such as these are important sources of fat for human as well as livestock consumption.

Animals and birds, like plants, can convert excess carbohydrate into fat. If an individual eats more carbohydrate than is required for the muscular work of the day, part of the excess will be stored as fat. In the case of budgerigars, if we feed a high percentage of oats to birds in a fairly restricted flight cage for a period of a month, then the fat deposits will begin to be apparent.

Mineral salts

In addition to carbohydrates, proteins and fat, all of which are organic substances, certain chemicals must be mentioned without which our birds could not survive since they constitute about 6 per cent of their bodies. The principal ones are calcium, phosphorus, potassium, sulphur, iron, copper, manganese, zinc, iodine, cobalt and fluorine.

CALCIUM

About 99 per cent of the body calcium is contained in the skeletal structure of the birds, plus about 1 per cent in circulation round the body principally for absorption by the shell gland in the case of female birds. Certain factors must be kept in mind when one considers some of the items currently used in budgerigar diets.

1 The total amount of calcium present from all the components of the diet.
2 Certain factors that assist the absorption of calcium, namely
   a vitamin D
   b protein
3 Certain factors that interfere and block the absorption of calcium, namely
   a fats in excess
   b phytic acid (e.g. brown bread given in excess)

The presence in the diet of Vitamin D, or its formation by sun action in the skin, assists absorption of calcium from foodstuffs in the digestive system. This is also facilitated by the presence of protein in the digestive system. The small percentage in the blood is necessary to avoid the loss of muscle tone and to complete the normal process of blood clotting when required and the controlling gland for the correct level of calcium is the parathyroid gland. A shortage of calcium is a contributory factor causing soft shelled eggs.

PHOSPHORUS

Phosphorus is responsible for maintaining the constancy of the body fluids; is a major component, with calcium, of bones and plays an essential part in the complicated chemistry by which the body obtains energy from food. It can be found in grain and oyster shell and is therefore abundant in budgerigar diets.

POTASSIUM

Potassium is similar in behaviour to common salt except that instead of remaining free in the body fluids it is retained within the cells of the tissues and the blood corpuscles. It is collected by the kidneys and any surplus is excreted in the urine. It can be described as a body fluid regulator, responsible at the same time for correct muscular functioning. A deficiency would be apparent by muscular weakness and mental apathy, but it is highly unlikely to occur since it is abundant in basic budgerigar diets.

SULPHUR

Minute quantities of sulphur are needed regularly and any food containing methionine and cystine in fair amounts will also contain sulphur. This is another body regulator and since feathers are composed mainly of protein, and cystine is an important building factor, a shortage of cystine with its sulphur content must result in inadequate feathering.

SODIUM

Sodium chloride, or in other words common salt, is a mineral that has a direct effect on nutrition. It is another regulator forming about 0·9 per cent of the body fluid. Essential for life and obtainable for birds in the form of bread or oats, any excess build up is excreted in the urine via the kidneys.

CHLORINE

This mineral is found combined with sodium and hydrogen and is a component of gastric juice, a blood regulator and also a component of urine. Also found in ordinary salt and therefore obtainable from oats and bread.

IRON

Iron is of great importance in nutrition and its absence is a common cause of ill health. A bird, or any living animal, that is deficient in iron is said to be anaemic since the amount of circulating haemoglobin in the blood is reduced. The result of this would appear as fatigue and breathlessness in the bird. Foods rich in iron are wholemeal bread, eggs, oats and meats, particularly liver. In green foods, spinach is a particularly well-known source, and by comparison to, say, cabbage contains five times as much iron.

IODINE

Iodine is a component of one gland of the body namely the thyroid, and while this subject is dealt with in more detail under the heading of diseases, it is important to remember that a dietary shortage of iodine may occur at any time and research on the thyroid glands of budgerigars in recent years has pinpointed the fact that many studs have suffered from this deficiency. Sources of iodine are grain grown in iodine rich soils and iodine blocks sold to the fancy for the specific purpose of countering any deficiency. Also there is a large percentage in the fish oils used as food supplements.

MAGNESIUM

Although needed only in small amounts, this is again one of those substances vital to life. Under biological experiments where magnesium is artificially withdrawn, life is quickly brought to a stop. Most of the body's store of magnesium is present in the bones in combination with phosphorus but it is required, in addition to bone building, for muscle activity, normal growth and for correct functioning of the blood and nervous systems. Magnesium is present in all grains and vegetables.

MANGANESE

Manganese plays a part in the release of energy in the cells during the combustion of fuel compounds obtained from food. Lack of this mineral causes reduced hatchability. Egg shell strength is also decreased to some extent. There is generally sufficient manganese in grain to supply budgerigar requirements.

Vitamins

This is a group of essential elements in food, but in recent years of budgerigar feeding there is good evidence to suggest that far too much stress has been placed on this subject. Too many fanciers have drawn incorrect conclusions from the information available to them.

New vitamins are being tested under laboratory control daily. A vitamin is one of a class of substances existing in minute quantities in natural foods and necessary to normal growth and feeding. Certain vitamins are soluble in water, others soluble in fat. Some are destroyed by heat, sunlight and age and others by rancidity. The absence of vitamins produces diseases, and an excess of vitamins causes grave problems. They are necessary only in minute quantities, yet it has become common to give them far in excess of the normal levels.

VITAMIN A

Functions

Vitamin A is needed for the correct functioning of the cells of the body, but the exact way it works is so far not clearly understood. It is absolutely necessary for all growing animals and birds; it is concerned with the growth of bones and is also necessary for the health of the skin and feathers. Vitamin A also has a bearing on the cornea (the outer surface) of the eye and the respiratory tract. It is known for its ability to work with a pigment on the light sensitive area of the eye, the retina, so that the eyes are able to function in a dim light.

Properties

Vitamin A is soluble in fats, therefore *not* soluble in water. It is stable at boiling temperature yet spoils with age if exposed to the air. The body stores it very readily in the liver.

Sources

Vitamin A activity is usually expressed in terms of 'international units'. This is a convenient method of denoting the biological activity of the vitamin in animal foods and, in the case of vegetable foods, of the carotene content. In this latter group, as a general guide, the carotene content of green vegetables runs roughly parallel to the degree of darkness of the leaves. For example there is a higher vitamin activity in spinach and watercress, by comparison to the white hearts of cabbage and lettuce.

Note: An international unit is the activity of 0·3 micrograms, i.e. 0·3 ten thousandths of a gram, of the pure chemical Vitamin A as it occurs in animal foods.

From the table opposite it will be quickly realized that the fish oil group is the most highly nutritious source available, but of course cod liver oil, which is the most widely used product, does contain another vital vitamin, Vitamin D. The part played by cod liver oil in the welfare of mothers and young children is well known and needs no further explanation.

TABLE IV

EXAMPLES OF VITAMIN A ACTIVITY OF CERTAIN FOODS

(international units per oz.)

Halibut Liver Oil	600,000	Spinach	1,500
Cod Liver Oil	30,000	Watercress	500
Other fish (average)	40	Cabbage	85
Sheep liver	6,000	Orange	50
Eggs	280	Nuts	0
Milk	30	Bread	0
Carrots	4,000		

Vitamin A in excess

When eaten in excess Vitamin A accumulates in the body, primarily in the liver. It can be stored in the muscular tissues as well and if consumed by birds may be acutely toxic, to the extent that symptoms of 'going light' may well be apparent (see page 162). It is important to remember that halibut liver oil contains nearly twenty times the amount of international units, by comparison to cod liver oil. Lack of appetite, unhealthy feather growths and swelling over the bones of the legs and feet are all symptomatic of Vitamin A toxicity.

Vitamin A deficiency (see page 165 – deficiency diseases).

VITAMIN B GROUP

This is a fairly large group of vitamins which combine to produce good health in all living animals. There are however certain members of this group which are of particular interest to us and these are:

Vitamin B_1 referred to as aneurin and sometimes thiamine.
Vitamin B_6 found in pyridoxine.
Vitamin B_{12} sold commercially as 'Cytacon'.
Riboflavin   previously called vitamin B_2
Niacin   found in nicotinic acid nicotinamide.

Vitamin B_1 (Thiamine, Aneurin)

This is very soluble in water, destroyed by heat and also destroyed by the presence of an alkali. Its function is to form part of an enzyme which controls the energy release from carbohydrates, which as we now know is one of the main sources of physical energy. It is not stored very easily by the body and although its deficiency will be dealt with in a later chapter, suffice to say at this stage that its absence from the diet causes the disease beri-beri in human beings. Although it is widely distributed in foods, it is only found in rich quantity in the germ of seeds and dried yeast.

Vitamin B_6

Vitamin B_6 plays an important part in the conversion of the amino acid, tryptophan, into niacin, but evidence to suggest that animals suffer harm from an inadequate supply is not proven. Chicks which suffer from muscular twitching and convulsions may be suffering from its absence but it is very unlikely, as one of the richest natural sources is seed grain.

Vitamin B_{12}

The chemical name for this vitamin is cyanocobalamin and it is sold by chemists under the name of Cytacon. It is an extremely active vitamin known in budgerigars to reduce their habit of eating their own droppings; however, there is no certainty that this is a wise habit to reduce, since it is quite natural to them. Since Vitamin B_{12} is present in livers and milk those fanciers who give foods containing these two items do not need to administer Cytacon in the water. To those who do use Cytacon, its high activity means the dosage has to be minute and any quantities as large as a teaspoonful per pint of water may cause uncountable problems. Cytacon is used in people to counteract a hitherto incurable disease known as pernicious anaemia and in zoos animals which lose their appetites and do not respond to their favourite foods are given a Vitamin B_{12} injection to stimulate their interest.

Riboflavin

Like Vitamin B_1, this is soluble in water and also has the same sort of function in bringing about the release of energy from carbohydrates. Although it has a similar function to B_1, its absence will check the growth of chicks very quickly. It is found in animal and vegetable foods such as milk and dried yeast and also greenfoods, and of course provided the wheat in bread is not highly milled, wholemeal bread is a very good source.

Niacin

This is another water soluble vitamin which functions very similarly to Vitamin B_1 and riboflavin. Lack of niacin in areas where people eat a poor monotonous diet, particularly if largely maize, gives rise to the disease pellagra. Rich sources are dried yeast and malt and also grain, so there is little likelihood of birds suffering from deficiency.

VITAMIN C

Vitamin C, unlike the other groups so far described, occurs in significant amounts in only two classes of food namely fresh green foods and fruit. It is lost very easily when heated and lack of adequate amounts give rise to scurvy. The body is not capable of storing it and excesses are excreted quickly. Normal chicks are born with sufficient Vitamin C to last them a few months, but if not supplied after that period their feet swell, breathing is difficult, they appear to be in undue pain when handled and their eyes dilate continuously when handled. In general they are very weak but respond within two or three days to any Vitamin C administered. The various types of green foods are discussed later in this book. For some years there was no evidence to suggest that extra Vitamin C consumed by people provided protection against infections, but recently there has been evidence to recommend a slightly higher intake of Vitamin C. Blackcurrants and rose hips are high in Vitamin C content, but be careful if using these in syrup form for birds, as if given in excess the syrup tends to scour the lower gut of the bird and cause troublesome intestinal disorders.

VITAMIN D

This is a vitamin of special importance since it is vital for the correct growth of bones. If in insufficient amounts in the body of a chick, the two minerals calcium and phosphorus do not combine correctly to form hard bones, with the results that the bird suffers from rickets, leg deformities become apparent and there is often evidence of permanently twisted wings.

Like Vitamin A, this vitamin is fat soluble and can be stored by the body. It can be acquired in two ways, either from fish oils, like cod liver oil, or by exposure to the ultra-violet rays of the sun, the rays converting a substance known as '7 dehydro-cholesterol' into Vitamin D.

If Vitamin D is provided in excessive amounts, there are definite harmful results; the chicks will suffer from loss of appetite, wasting, vomiting and constipation. In bad cases even more serious symptoms resulting in death have been recorded, leaving a completely baffled fancier searching for the cause.

VITAMIN E

Often called the anti-sterility vitamin, this important vitamin is found in very high concentration in the fatty part of most grains and wheat germ oil is a particularly active source. Animal fats however do not contain very much of this vitamin. It is important to note that whereas in people ill health due to shortage of Vitamin E has never been proven, in the case of animals and birds it can raise serious problems (see page 167). The vitamin has one other important property in that it is valuable as an anti-oxidant in foods, to protect fats from becoming rancid.

Practical Feeding

The criteria for a healthy well nourished budgerigar should be as follows: good development of the skeletal structure, skin and beak, good muscle tone, a steady gain in weight coupled with first-class feather growth from about seven days old, a bright active outlook on life with good resistance to infection and a good appetite. Given all these factors, a bird should be able to withstand numerous exhibitions in the course of the show season, yet be capable at the end of reproducing two full rounds of chicks under artificial conditions.

The controlling factor in achieving this end with every bird in the stud is food; the quality and quantity of feedstuffs, plus added vitamins, is the difference between success or failure in this hobby.

The basic diet

Any budgerigar will survive in a healthy condition if fed four items, these being seeds of a specific blend, water, cuttlefish bone and grit. The serious breeder however cannot expect to reproduce stock of any consequence on such bare essentials. On the other side of the coin, it is possible to overdo it by giving excess additives, usually in the form of vitamins, which give rise to a condition known as hypervitaminosis. The symptoms of this appear to indicate an infectious disease, rather than a nutritional error (see Chapter 14). Seeds vary in their nutritional content depending on the ground in which they grew and their degree of ripeness when harvested, so results in the breeding room can also vary as a direct result of these factors. The basic diet therefore is inadequate and must be added to in moderation so that the ideal food balance is obtained. If diseases are encountered, then the stud or group of birds affected are usually suffering from an imbalance caused by an incorrect diet.

Establishing a system

Start from the outset a feeding programme file in which you will keep a complete record of every item given to the stud and the proportion in which it is given. If a series of good seasons is encountered naturally one is pleased, but suddenly one year all manner of things occur and a bad season becomes a reality. If a notebook has been correctly kept it will be simple to check your feeding programme to see whether you over-looked a certain vitamin or introduced a compound which another fancier had recommended. If the diet is unchanged and the sources of seed have remained constant, then the cause of the problem must be elsewhere. However in 90 per cent of cases the answer will be nutritional; your feeding notebook is a vital factor.

You are now ready to evolve a programme of feeding for your stud which has to be divided into two sections, the breeding season and non-breeding season. Birds, like any other creatures, have high and low peaks, in the case of budgerigars shown by good and poor condition. If fed a high vitamin supplemented diet all the year round, their bodies rebel, resulting in loose droppings of variable colours and shapes, the birds take on a permanently chilled appearance and lose weight. These are symptoms of what fanciers term 'going light'. Your stock therefore has to be built up to a pitch of high condition as breeding is about to start, and allowed to come back to normal level once the last chicks have been reared. With these two seasonal changes in mind a suitable feeding programme can be evolved.

The essential nutrients which any ration must provide are:

Water
Starch and sugar
Protein
Fats and oils
Vitamins
Minerals

Water is vital to the diet since the body of a bird contains 60 per cent and the egg 65 per cent. Lack of water retards growth and its absence leads to death in a short period. Water is vital also for the absorption of essential nutrients and for removing poisonous waste products via the kidneys. Lastly it acts as a lubricant for the bone joints and maintains the blood in its correct balance.

Starch and sugar are the two means of supplying rapid energy to any living creature and in the case of the budgerigar this is largely obtained from the seed intake. Canary seed and oats contain 60 per cent starch while millet has 70 per cent.

Protein, more than any other factor, plays an important role in reproducing top-class exhibition birds. Seed of course also contains protein, canary seed and oats have 17 per cent and 15 per cent respectively while millet has only 12 per cent. The food substances with the highest protein content are meats, milk and eggs and certain human baby milk compounds are excellent sources worth consideration. The late Jack Fisher of Repton, an authority on nutrition, maintained that the quantity of protein from seed was adequate but of low grade quality, the important factor being the amount of protein that is easily assimilated. There are now excellent compounds made by the seed manufacturers, similar to the insectile foods given to softbills, which possess a high percentage of protein. The wider the range of protein offered to your birds the better your results will be.

Fats are supplied in the form of seed since most contain around 10 per cent, while oats of course are known to be an excellent form of building up fat in birds, especially if their activity is curtailed at the same time.

Under the general heading of additives come all the extra requirements that are needed to produce full nests of pedigree sized budgerigars. These can take all forms but contain a host of vitamins and mineral salts which can be given in any easy way. Both vitamins and minerals are essential to avoid ill health but are best given in a natural form if possible. For example greenfood Vitamin C is preferable to a soluble concentrated Vitamin C such as rose hip syrup.

A recommended diet

Below are two good basic programmes of feeding for the breeding and non-breeding seasons. After trying these diets in an individual stud, you may decide to vary certain items; whatever those items happen to be, experiment first with only a few pairs of birds, at the outside a quarter of the stud. Then if results are poor you can establish the cause. Do not experiment with more than one item at a time or the cause of the good or bad results cannot be established.

Non-breeding season

Canary seed forms 80 per cent of the seed intake. There are a number of grades of the grass phalaris canariensis which form the staple diet of budgerigars, grown in various parts of the world. In order of preference these are Spanish, Mazagan, Moroccan, Turkish, Australian and

English. The order of preference is based on size, Spanish canary being the largest, coupled with availability and cost factors. The degree of ripening is also critical and it is therefore to be expected that English canary seed must for this reason be different from the Mediterranean equivalents. Mazagan is the seed most commonly used.

Millets, which come as white millets or yellow millets, comprise a further 10 per cent of the seed mixture. This is the seed of the grass panicum miliaceum and can grow well in areas of poor soil and low rainfall. It grows to a height of twelve feet in some areas and when harvested is marketed to fanciers as loose seed or in the unthreshed form of millet sprays. The main sources of millet are Italy, China, Australia and India, with a lower grade Japanese millet becoming more popular as an extra.

Choose as many forms of millet as possible from different growing areas, mixing together the white, yellow and Japanese types. In addition, give millet sprays of different origins to the flights twice per week.

To the canary seed and mixed millets add 5 per cent clipped oats. Oats can be fattening and therefore form a small part of the diet but can be obtained whole or without a husk. In the latter form the oat is referred to as a groat and because of its absorbent nature is useful for those who wish to give pure cod liver oil.

Oats can of course be soaked in water, germinated and fed separately to the stock. In the process of germination the seed produces an enzyme called diastase which is of benefit. The normal method of soaking is quite simple, a quantity of oats is placed in a colander and immersed in water for twelve hours. On removal they must be well rinsed, allowed to drain and left for twenty four hours. After rinsing again they can then be given to the birds or allowed a further day during which time the young shoots should emerge. All budgerigars love to eat these. Oats must be fed sparingly and must be very well rinsed before administering

The remaining 5 per cent of the seed intake is what is termed 'tonic' seed. This is supplied by the trade under this name and while it is not an essential requirement, it adds a little extra variety to the diet since it is a mixture of Japanese millet, niger seed, linseed and dried vegetable leaves. The birds do not always eat the linseed but it assists the process of the moult and promotes that lovely sheen on the feathering of the stock.

So to summarize, the seed mixture for the non-breeding season is as follows:

Mazagan canary seed	80 per cent
Mixed millets	10 per cent
Clipped oats	5 per cent
Tonic seed	5 per cent

To this mixture add two supplements to the diet, namely a cod liver oil emulsion referred to as 'B.O.B.' emulsion and a purified yeast powder.

Take an ordinary biscuit tin and partially fill it with the seed mixture until it contains 3–4 lb. seed. To this, add $\frac{1}{2}$ teaspoonful cod liver oil emulsion per pound of seed and thoroughly shake the tin until every grain is coated. Leave the mixture in the tin for a minimum of twelve hours. By this time the emulsion will have been absorbed into the mixture so that it is free running again, instead of sticky. Do be accurate with the dosage, it is most important. Then add the treated seed to an equal proportion of dry, untreated seed and mix. Mix in the yeast powder thoroughly at the rate of $\frac{1}{2}$ teaspoonful to 8 lb. seed and the mixture is ready for feeding.

The cod liver oil is given because it contains the essential Vitamins A and D and is the finest way of administering iodine. The yeast provides a source of protein plus a natural form of the Vitamin B complex. Iron, copper, cobalt, manganese are present to provide essential mineral salts and also there is a blending of calcium and phosphorus.

Water should be replenished each day, the receptacles being cleaned at the same time. If possible, all consumable water should be boiled and cooled since, for reasons I am not entirely able to explain, this seems to improve results. Whether the trace elements in water or the dissolved solids have an adverse effect on small birds is uncertain, but boiling the water reduces problems noticeably. I usually have a two pint jug in the aviary to which I add two drops of Abidec and one teaspoonful of Cytacon. These are obtainable from any chemist and are again vitamin supplements, blended in the right proportions. Abidec is a source of Vitamins A, D, B group and C, this source of Vitamin C being sufficient to allow you to dispense with green food if you wish. Other sources of Vitamin C are rose hip syrup and blackcurrant. Cytacon provides Vitamin B_{12}.

Cuttlefish bone and grit must both be provided at all times. Cuttlefish bone is the 'relic' structure of the cuttlefish which strangely enough in life does not serve any structural or protective purpose; it is composed of calcium carbonate and is the vital source of calcium for budgerigars. Grit is essential for the correct functioning of the gizzard, in which particles of grit are used to grind up the grains to digestible proportions. Do not fall into the trap of looking at the grit dish, observing that it is still half full after perhaps a week or so, and leaving it. Budgies are selective when it comes to grit and if the particles are not suitable they are rejected. Therefore whatever the appearance of the grit after a certain time you must discard it and replenish it with a fresh supply. Only by doing this can you expect to avoid digestive problems.

Choose coarse grade grits of sea washed origin in preference to those from inland sources, because there is always a risk of contamination from the latter. To the grits, which may be mixed from different areas if so desired, add oystershell grit, in the proportion 1 part oystershell to 5 parts grit. Oystershell is taken very readily and is of great benefit.

Breeding season
The only changes to the diet that need to be made in the breeding season are an increase of certain items. The Abidec should be increased to ten drops to two pints of water and the seed should be 100 per cent treated with cod liver oil emulsion.

Many breeders like to offer a mixture of wholemeal bread and milk, the bread being cut into cubes and sprinkled with glucose sugar. This is given to each breeding pair on alternate nights, alternating with a small amount of sprouted oats. Neither must be left for more than a day to go stale. This mixture assists the new born chicks to get a good start in life. The parents become so used to it that many breeding pairs wait for the arrival of one item or the other. The only difficulty is maintaining the routine for two rounds of chicks, without break. It is easy to forget one night, then the adults will feed an inadequate amount to their chicks and extra problems ensue.

GREENFOOD
Those who have a regular supply of greenfood available from an un-contaminated source throughout the year are fortunate. The majority of us are not so lucky. It is possible occasionally to find a good source but with top-grade exhibition birds, particularly if you have a big stud, there are always risks associated with windborne weedkillers and fertilizers, plus the chance that the greenfood has been fouled by animals. There is however no substitute for greenfood for your stud, so gather it if you can, wash it thoroughly and feed it to the stock in the early morning. In the evening remove and throw away any uncon-sumed leaves. When seeding grasses are in season, these will always be safe to give and the birds will relish them.

There is one type of greenfood to be favoured more than any other and that is chickweed. This is a low growing, ground spreading plant with a small, white, starlike flower and it is peculiar inasmuch as it will only grow in abundance on very good soil. Perhaps this is the reason it is found in quantity on farms and nurseries. It is quite safe to give and a first class food given daily when the stock is breeding. If you want to give greens but do not have a regular source, then I recommend you plant perpetual spinach at set intervals. Spinach is excellent, a couple of small leaves per day to the breeding pairs being sufficient and pro-rata to the flights.

Many greenfoods are astringent in their action, as well as acting as a tonic. Others are purging especially if given in excess. Shepherds' purse is an example of the former and dandelion and groundsel easily cause diarrhoea. Lettuce and cabbage are quite safe provided the leaves are fresh, while carrots are an excellent alternative in the winter months if the greens are frosted. The general rule with all greenfoods and root crops is to give them in moderation. Not to give any for some months and then suddenly to give an excessive quantity is to ask for trouble.

Consistency

Whatever you decide to feed and from wherever the seed orginates, make up your mind when you are satisfied and stick to it. The fancier who is supplied by a well-known retailer, then forgets to order and dashes down to the pet shop for an interim supply, will pay the penalty when the season is under way. Order well in advance and even if the price increases do not be tempted to alter to a cheaper grade. This is false economy as the birds will suffer.

10 *An opaline cinnamon grey green cock with good head quality and depth of mask.*

9 *Skyblue cock with a top class head mask and spots.*

11 *A normal grey cock showing good width between the eyes.*

13 Dominant skyblue pied—Best Pied
at the Budgerigar Society Club
Show, Leicester, 1973.

14 Opaline grey cock—Best Budgerigar
in Show at the National Exhibition of
Cage Birds, London, 1972.

15 (far left) The
red mite, anterior
view (x 200
magnification).

16 (left) The red
mite, ventral view
showing the blood
sucking proboscis
(x 1000
magnification).

7. The Science of Breeding

Genetics

The first large-scale and controlled experiments on heredity were carried out on plants by an Austrian monk named Gregor Johann Mendel (1822–84) in Central Europe. These experiments were carried out using sweet peas, which are easily distinguished by differences in height, shape, colour of their seeds and other features. Initially Mendel chose one plant with round seeds, and another with seeds that had a wrinkled coat. These he crossed and all the resultant seeds were round. He allowed these hybrids (a hybrid is a new breed produced by the union of unlike parents) to self fertilize and produce more seeds. From an analysis of these, a ratio of three round seeds to one wrinkled seed emerged. Further experiments proved that one-third of the round seeds behaved like the original round seeds of the grandparents while the remainder resembled those seeds which formed their hybrid parents. It therefore appeared that one-half of the offspring of hybrid parents will resemble their parents and the other half will have equal chances of resembling one of the grandparents. The first generation (referred to scientifically as the first filial, or F_1, generation) resembled the round rather than the wrinkled parent. Certain characteristics are therefore *dominant*. The wrinkled characteristic was subordinate and as such is referred to as *recessive*. In budgerigars all recessive characteristics are referred to as 'split' characteristics; they are written after an oblique stroke following the visible colour. For example a light green/blue/opaline appears green but has split recessive blue and opaline characteristics.

The understanding of these basic principals can help the breeder of budgerigars considerably.

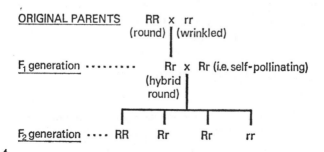

ORIGINAL PARENTS   RR x rr
                  (round) (wrinkled)

F_1 generation · · · · · · · · ·   Rr x Rr (i.e. self-pollinating)
                  (hybrid
                  round)

F_2 generation · · · · RR   Rr   Rr   rr

To understand breeding and the creation of life it is necessary to begin with one cell. A cell is a unit of life and the descendant of another cell. In plants, each cell has a cell wall which gives a honeycomb appearance, but in animals and birds such a wall is not present since it is the contents that constitute the cell, which comprises a central nucleus surrounded by a complex substance called cytoplasm. It is the nucleus that is principally involved in cell division.

There are two types of cell division, the commonest of which is mitosis. The resting nucleus contains thread-like structures called chromosomes and on these are placed the innumerable hereditary factors or *genes*, which are handed down from parents to offspring, rather like a long row of dots on a rod. When a new life is created one sperm containing a nucleus with its own set of genes penetrates the outer covering of the egg in the female. The male nucleus divides into two half cells, half of the chromosomes going into one half cell and half into the other. The female cell also becomes two half cells. The uniting of two half cells, one from the sperm and one from the egg, forms one cell and each chromosome finds its own partner from its opposite cell. In this tiny new cell is the blue-print of the future budgerigar. The sex, colour, feather length and texture, type, size of spots and head are all contained within this cell. Fertilization has been effected.

Genes in general remain unchanged generation after generation, the basic characteristics being commuted in many different ways resulting in differences amongst the species. The process of inbreeding endeavours to collect the desirable genes together and funnel them into the near perfect specimens we all desire. Genes are rather like two packs of cards mixed together, perfection is only realized when you turn up eight consecutive aces in one hand.

Breeders will often hear the word 'mutation' quoted. Mutations, when they occur, are generally harmful and are the result of a pair of genes which have become altered in some way so that the character of the genes is also altered. Not all these alterations are favourable since deformities may arise, sometimes in horrific forms, but a good example of a mutation which could possibly take place in the future would be the appearance of a red budgerigar.

The Reproductive System

Females

In female birds, during their embryonic stage, two rudimentary ovaries exist but normally the left ovary develops fully upon maturity while the right atrophies. The ovary is situated in front of the left kidney and in the non-breeding season is quite small. When breeding starts it enlarges quickly and the eggs that are produced resemble a tiny bunch of grapes, the number varying with the species.

The eggs are released from the ovary in yolk form. Technically they

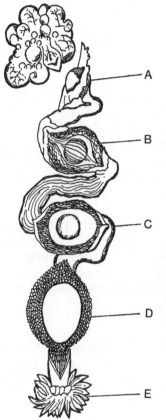

The reproductive tract of the hen budgerigar

A *Infundibulum.*

B *Magnum: thick albumen is secreted around the yolk, taking three to four hours.*

C *Isthmus: secretion of the shell membrane takes about one hour.*

D *Shell gland: this receives the albumen during the first four to eight hours. The shell is deposited around the membrane within about twenty hours.*

E *The vagina moves the egg through the cloaca.*

then enter the body cavity, but nature has induced the top end of the oviduct (egg tube) to act as a receiver for them. This open end is termed the infundibular orifice. Once the eggs pass into the top part of the oviduct, the magnum, they are subjected to secretions from the walls of the oviduct which lay down the 'egg white' that surrounds the yolk. First of all the gelatinous threads, or chalazae, which ultimately suspend the yolk in the middle of the shell, are deposited, and further down the oviduct the remaining three layers of 'white' albumen are acquired. These processes take three to four hours to complete. In the next section of the oviduct, the isthmus, the membrane which surrounds the white is formed in about one hour before the egg enters the fourth area, the shell gland. In this glandular section, over a period of some twenty-four hours, the shell is deposited about the membrane. After this the completed egg moves into the final vaginal passage before being laid through the cloaca to the outside. In budgerigars, eggs are laid on alternate days. The average round is five or six eggs though larger numbers, in excess of twelve, have frequently been recorded.

Males

The male sex glands or testes are situated close to the body wall under the backbone and their size varies according to the season. Normally the right testis is the larger. Each testis consists of a series of coiled tubes in which the spermatozoa or male fertilizing cells are formed. These tiny tubes are called the 'seminiferous tubules'. Arising from each testis is a short tube called the epididymis where the sperm are stored, this leads directly to a duct called the vas deferens down which the sperm are passed to the cloaca.

Each sperm comprises a small head, containing the nucleus, followed by a long whiplike tail. Upon completion of mating the sperm swim up, assisted by movement in the female tract, towards the infundibulum; there, if one meets an infertile egg and penetrates it, the egg is then fertilized. A chemical change in the egg prevents further penetration by other sperm.

Inbreeding and Line Breeding

In genetics any matings that take place within a family as closely as first cousins are considered to be inbreeding and anything more distant to be line breeding. The word line is used to mean family.

Inbreeding from the stockman's point of view is carried out with an intention to purify the stock. The mating of either parent with their offspring, brother to sister, or first cousin to first cousin are all methods of inbreeding and these are the methods at the breeder's disposal for improving strains and individual families by the concentration of their genes or characteristics.

Many breeders are unsure when to start inbreeding, if at all. The late Dr M. D. S. Armour stated that periodic inbreeding is essential if genetic purity is desired, culminating in improvement in show quality amongst other features. By choosing the vital points in related birds one can concentrate these desirable features over several generations until the ideal points have been achieved.

Breeders are often concerned about inbreeding, fearing that after many generations their birds may become sterile and prized lines may die out. Provided birds are selected for excellent traits and included amongst those the trait for virility, all will be well for a maximum of four consecutive generations. In the U.S.A. brother to sister pairings in mice have been experimented upon for over a hundred generations with no harmful results because the virility factor had been taken into account. Inbreeding tends to make pure lines which once established reach a point when it is useless to proceed further. This stage necessitates introducing a superior outcross, which will also make up for any possible lack of fertility which may have developed. In mice the quantity produced from each generation gives a large number of offspring from which to choose the ideal pairings. In budgerigars this may not be the case, therefore inevitably some undesirable pairings may be effected with subsequent loss of fertility. For four consecutive generations inbreeding can be employed; subsequent inbred generations could be adversely affected.

The aim of inbreeding should be to eliminate undesirable features and to 'double-up' desirable features.

To illustrate the above statement one of the great inbreeding experiments was carried out by Dr D. B. Jones. He reasoned that if he could inbreed two lines of maize plants until all the defects had been eliminated he could then cross these two lines together, which ought to produce a superb plant. This he did for nine generations. In this process he gradually lost size, but each line was so inbred that they retained only the superior qualities, although they were not as large as the original plant. Finally, subsequent to the ninth generations in each line, he crossed the two lines together and the results were the finest plants ever seen and their yield was 120 per cent greater.

With this illustration in mind, you will see that inbreeding can be applied to budgerigars by the astute breeder to great advantage, though the breeder must have an experienced eye to know exactly the desirable points of a bird; this in itself requires years of experience. Added to this, any one bird, however brilliant in quality, contains hidden features and only by judicious inbreeding can one find out whether those features are of use or otherwise.

After each inbreeding season the desirable birds are retained. The remainder are excluded irrespective of their parentage. Pedigrees must inevitably be utilized throughout the process of inbreeding to follow the desired lines accurately. Then, every few generations an outcross is brought in to assist in a particular point which is obviously not going to appear (e.g. depth of mask). Then we inbreed still further until the whole line has the feature established. Those who avoid inbreeding, and follow a policy of buying perpetual outcrosses, will always have a non-uniform stock which cannot be identified as individualistic. In addition the number of show winners produced will be very limited relative to the size of the stud, whereas a few years of calculated inbreeding would produce a whole series of good open show specimens.

Ideal matings
Assuming then you are an experienced breeder and you have a collection of birds which while acceptable to a degree are not uniformly of the highest quality, how then do you proceed to improve this group and what can be considered the best matings?

The first factor to decide is which birds if any are prepotent? This means which strains (lines) in your aviary have dominant characteristics, so that regardless to whom they are mated they seem to produce quality specimens with their own dominant characteristics?

This decided, a programme of inbreeding or line breeding where necessary can be instituted. If you have no prepotent birds then they will have to be purchased if you are determined to succeed. You now embark on this programme, ensuring that no two birds with the same faults are ever mated together. A full analysis of each bird must be made, not only of its visual features but of its habits. For example some birds have the irritating habit of having marvellous head qualities in the flight which promptly disappear when the bird is placed in the show cage. Such a factor has to be bred out. Some of the most successful matings have come from grandmother to grandson, grandfather to grand-daughter, half brother to half sister when the common parent is outstanding, uncle to niece and aunt to nephew. Brother to sister can be used but it must be remembered they cannot add any new characteristics. To show up the faults quickly as well as the good points, mother to son and father to daughter pairings can be used, though preferably these two pairings should only be made when the good qualities far outweigh the faults.

Breeding out faults

It is a good idea to concentrate one's attention on a particular fault for as many seasons as it takes to eliminate it, though it must be recognized that many faults arise from the recessive genes rather than the dominant ones. Should this be the case and a fault has bred into the strain, it is important to know how to correct it. An immediate outcross will result in its disappearance, unless it is a dominant gene. If the best chicks are chosen and mated back to their parent or grandparent, the one used to correct the fault, then the subsequent generations may have half the progeny with the correct point. From then on one selects and eliminates. The alternative is to use outcrosses all the time to correct faults, by which one brings in other hidden faults from those purchases.

Conclusions

A pedigree file and a card-index system in the aviary is essential and this must be kept up to date if any serious attempts at close breeding are to meet with success. Examples of suitable record cards are shown on the following pages.

Foundation birds must be chosen with great care and as much background information as possible about each individual must be obtained from the breeder. It is advisable in the first instance to choose perhaps two leading breeders whose strains are known to overlap. Look at as many birds as you can in the line of each foundation bird before purchasing and note all you are told.

Never contemplate inbreeding unless the stock is absolutely sound physically and, where necessary, stock must be culled vigorously if success is to be achieved. Any faulted birds that are kept may be accidentally used to the detriment of the stud. If necessary *give* them away.

BREEDING RECORD

COCK   HEN   COLOURED   PAIR No.

SEX LINKAGE EXPECTATION   DUE TO HATCH

DATE EGGS LAID	DATE HATCHED	TRANSFERRED	COLOUR	RING No.	REMARKS

Breeding record card

SHOW RECORD

Name of Show	Date	Judge	Award	Specials

Show record card

Identification Ring ....   Index No. ....

PEDIGREE

Colour ....   Sex ....   Ring Number ....

Date Hatched ....

Parents	Grandparents	Great Grandparents
		Cock ....
	Cock	Ring No. ....
	Ring No.	Hen ....
Cock........................		Ring No. ....
Ring No.		Cock ....
	Hen	Ring No. ....
	Ring No.	Hen ....
		Ring No. ....
		Cock ....
	Cock	Ring No. ....
	Ring No.	Hen ....
Hen........................		Ring No. ....
Ring No.		Cock ....
	Hen	Ring No. ....
	Ring No........................	Hen ....
		Ring No. ....

Pedigree card

8. Colours and their Reproduction

The basic colours and their variations give an enormous range of colour combinations in the budgerigar species, which allows any intending exhibitor an excellent choice of specialization in the colour that appeals to him most. Budgerigars have been bred in all colours with the exceptions of black, brown and red, though many years ago it was reported that two red patched birds had occurred in an Australian aviary run on the colony breeding system. In addition to breeding one or more colours, sex-linked factors can be added which will be referred to later; the commonest of these are the opaline and cinnamon characteristics.

Before pairing birds for breeding it is important to have a thorough knowledge of colours and their reproduction. This knowledge once acquired is subsequently applied quite instinctively when choosing the various partners; it is rarely necessary thereafter to refer to the book. Years of experience by past breeders have confirmed the ideal matings to reproduce the finest budgerigars with the depth and even colour necessary in the exhibition bird. Initially breeders concentrated more on colour than quality, and even the top quality big headed cock of today with perfect type will soon be marked down if his colour is insipid and a departure from the B.S. Standard.

Normals and the sex-linked factors

The term, 'normal' is applied to a group of colours to differentiate them from the rarer combinations. The word normal relates to the markings of the light greens in the wild, which were the original budgerigars. The light green bird has a clear frontal to the top of the head, at which point barring takes over and proceeds down the back. The wings are evenly black and yellow throughout with no patches. Any bird with these characteristics, whatever its colour, is classed as a normal.

The sex-linked varieties comprise, either separately or in a combined form, opalines, cinnamons, red eyed varieties, and slates. The first three types are very common and only the slates are rarely seen today. Genetically, planned reproduction of the sex-linked varieties works in a different way from the usual handing down of characteristics. With these groups the sex chromosomes are controlled when birds are chosen for pairing. The kind of chick produced, and its sex, depends on the types of birds used for the sire and the dam. For example, a normal cock × sex-linked hen does not reproduce the same chicks as those from a sex-linked cock × normal hen.

How does sex-linkage work? Each cell contains a nucleus, and within this nucleus are chromosomes. On each chromosome are the genes. It is the genes which determine the character and nature of the progeny. The chromosomes are laid down in pairs and in budgerigars there are twenty five or more pairs in each nucleus. In each pair, one appears to be rod like, while the other resembles a dot; when fertilization is effected, one of each pair of chromosomes results in a chick possessing the full complement, half having been supplied by the cock and half by the hen. However, there is one pair of chromosomes which controls sex. In the cock these two chromosomes are identical and are called the x chromosomes or more accurately xx. The hen, however, has only one similar to the cock and one dissimilar. She is therefore composed of xy.

The point of sex-linkage becomes apparent when it is realized that the gene controlling the sex-linked feature is situated on the x chromosome. Cocks therefore, as they are xx, can carry the gene, for example cinnamon, on one chromosome or on both chromosomes or on neither. If on neither then the bird is a normal. If the cinnamon gene is on one of the ẋx then the bird will appear normal but carry the characteristic as a recessive factor (i.e. the normal cock is split for cinnamon). If the cinnamon gene is on both ẋẋ the bird will be visibly cinnamon. In the case of the hen she can be visibly cinnamon if the gene is on her ẋy chromosome, or she is non-cinnamon since the y chromosome cannot carry the gene. A hen can therefore under no circumstances be recessive for a sex-linked feature. A 'split opaline hen' is genetically quite impossible.

Bearing these facts about sex-linkage in mind, and remembering that although cinnamon is being used as an example the other sex-linked features can be substituted for cinnamon, the following table of pairings clarifies the pattern.

---

1. CINNAMON COCK ẋẋ—CINNAMON HEN ẋY
   = Cinnamon cocks   ẍẍ
      Cinnamon hens   ẋY

---

2. CINNAMON COCK ẍẍ—*NORMAL HEN XY
   = *Normal/cinnamon cocks ẋx
      Cinnamon hens   ẋY

---

3. *NORMAL COCK XX—CINNAMON HEN ẊY
  = *Normal/cinnamon cocks ẊX
   *Normal hens   XY

---

4. *NORMAL/CINNAMON COCK ẊX—*NORMAL HEN XY
  = *Normal cocks   XX ⎫
   *Normal/cinnamon cocks ẊX ⎬ Visually identical
   Cinnamon hens   ẊY ⎭
   *Normal hens   XY

---

5. *NORMAL/CINNAMON COCK ẊX—CINNAMON HEN ẊY
  = *Normal/cinnamon cocks ẊX
   Cinnamon cocks   ẌẊX
   *Normal hens   XY
   Cinnamon hens   ẊY

★ 'Normal' refers to ordinary varieties **in appearance** not sex-linked.

Under item four it will be noted that this pairing results in cocks which could be either split for cinnamon or non-cinnamon. Which they are can only be ascertained by subsequent breeding.

Light green

This is the original 'wild' colour found in Australia and probably there is no colour as eagerly sought after as a top class normal light green. This situation has arisen largely as a result of there being very few studs of pure light greens in existence. The only way to reproduce this colour is by mating light green to light green. Any departure from this and the progeny start to look paler and perhaps patchy. It is possible to breed good light greens by crossing light green to pure bred normal grey greens, preferably with no hidden factors, and this is the only reasonable alternative.

Dark green

This series is difficult to specialize in since dark green is a heterozygous colour. This means that paired to itself, it realizes dark green, olive and light green chicks with the dark green chicks usually being uneven in colour. Some of the better dark greens have resulted from a light green to dark green pairing.

Genetically dark green/blues are divided into two groups, type I and type II. Type I are produced from pairing a skyblue to an olive. Type II are produced from a mauve to light green pairing. When considering using a dark green/blue, it is necessary to understand into which category the bird falls, since type I birds are the best for skyblue reproduction and type II are ideal for cobalt and violet breeding. Used correctly the dark green can reproduce the appropriate blue series in a bright and deep colour.

The use of the violet is the finest way to produce dark greens with the true laurel colour required. Supporting evidence is that it is often difficult to differentiate between some poor dark greens and the darker type of light greens and in general both of these are useless on the show bench. As with many of the colours which are mentioned in this chapter, dark greens can be reproduced as good examples of their colour but by reason of the fact that one partner, say the violet, is one of the best in the country, it is still so far behind in head and type qualities to its mate that the pairing cannot be considered. A further example is mauve to dark green/blue type I. This is an ideal pairing in theory since a small percentage of dark green/blue type II birds of excellent colour will be bred in addition to olive/blues and cobalts. However quality mauve specimens are just not available.

Olive

This is another colour which has declined in recent years, mainly because of the popularity of the grey green from which it differs only slightly in body colour and cheek patches. The value of olives lies mainly in their production of cobalts and mauves. However it is a variety that anyone could concentrate on and produce a high quality stud, given a degree of determination; should such a stud materialize in the next decade, then most surely the owner would have no difficulty in disposing of his stock, for the demand would be high.

Olive × olive pairings are considered the best, the main aim being to obtain the same even colour that the grey greens in general possess. The difficulty, however, is obtaining olives of sufficiently high standard to start with; but a fancier prepared to seek out the best available birds over a few years could easily establish himself. Many years ago yellow olives were paired to dark greens to produce some excellent quality olives and of course olive × dark green will produce a percentage, though this pairing can be overdone.

Skyblue

The skyblue is the most popular of the blue series. The birds are in general smaller, more racy and have poorer head qualities than the green group. Skyblue hens of top quality are few and far between and if fanciers realized this point a little more they would perhaps not be so quick to part with moderate quality hens.

When pairing, skyblue × skyblue is satisfactory for one or two generations but one has to be careful not to lose too much size and colour. Eventually one has to 'dip into the green' and introduce preferably a quality light green into the series. One should preferably choose the best skyblue cock available and pair it to the best light green hen available, the resulting progeny being all light green/blues. The hen should be a buff light green (see page 59), if possible with that extra length of feather, head quality, size of spots and depth of mask the skyblue series lacks. These splits can subsequently be mated to the skyblues and upgrade not only their colour but their overall qualities. Should the chosen light green hen be herself split for blue, then so much the better. This 'dipping into the green' is one of the reasons the light green has declined because there is an unmistakable yellowing of the green colour in many light green/blues.

Another excellent pairing is skyblue × cobalt, as indeed is skyblue × dark green/blue type 1. The skyblue × cobalt pairing, however, is a pairing only for the advanced breeder since the colour qualities of both must be known for some generations back if the blues and cobalts bred are to be of sufficiently good depth of colour. It is very easy for the results to turn out patchy in both cases.

Cobalt

Like the dark greens, the cobalts are heterozygous. If two cobalts are mated together the resulting progeny will be 25 per cent mauve, 25 per cent skyblue and 50 per cent cobalt. (Skyblues are homozygous: when they are paired together 100 per cent skyblue progeny is the result.) In recent years cobalts of quality have been difficult to find; it is rare for a cobalt to be found Best Budgerigar in Show. This is in contrast to the pre-war and immediate post-war periods when they often took top honours.

The aim of every cobalt breeder is to obtain richness and evenness of colour, at the same time maintaining type and quality. Unfortunately one of the best matings is cobalt paired to mauve, yet the mauve itself has become rare in recent years on the show bench. Cobalt paired to cobalt, provided the birds themselves both have the correct depth of colour and no patchiness, can produce some excellent cobalts. This pairing is worth consideration but it is advisable that the first generation be paired to other colours when mature to avoid deterioration of the desired features. Skyblue to mauve will reproduce 100 per cent cobalts and will allow a wider choice to be made from the youngsters, but again the difficulty of obtaining a satisfactory high quality mauve arises.

It is advisable when breeding cobalts to confine your pairings to the blue series but it may be found necessary to 'dip into the green' again to maintain size and type. Should this be necessary, then the use of dark green/blue type I to cobalt or dark green/blue type II to skyblue may be the best solution, provided the dark greens themselves have quality cobalts in their ancestry in addition to being top class even coloured dark greens themselves. The reproduction of cobalts to champion open show quality is another field very much open to the enthusiastic specialist. We can but hope that one of these beautiful birds, with snow white cap and mask and with all the necessary exhibition 'punch', will grace the winner's stand in the near future.

Mauve

The colour of mauves is of utmost importance and a top quality mauve, though rare, would be invaluable in the breeding room. Unfortunately it is a colour that requires complete absence of patchiness if it is to be benched; since this is difficult to achieve, the colour has tended to fall by the wayside. The mauve has to compete in the same class with the skyblues and cobalts and consequently the variety is almost extinct as far as champion quality is concerned.

Mauves are best produced from olive/blue to mauve or olive/blue to cobalt pairings, though the use of the cobalt may tend to introduce flecking in the body colour. Immediately the problem referred to earlier recurs – exhibition standard olive/blues just do not exist at present.

Violet

Many breeders have set out to specialize in this glorious bird and the violets were of champion exhibition quality between 1947 and 1954. Since then they have declined somewhat. The true visual violet is a bird of intense colour and brilliance, yet only a handful of top exhibition birds have been seen. This is largely because it is not easy to breed large numbers of them. The violet is not a bird for the beginner; many experienced fanciers who have tried to specialize in violets have given up out of sheer frustration.

The best violet show specimens have resulted accidentally from some of the bigger studs where a dark characteristic runs through certain blue lines. So far the violet specialists have produced some wonderfully coloured birds but invariably they have lacked in head qualities and spots.

The factor which causes the blue series to have this rich colouring is dominant and consequently violets can be single or double factored. However it has to be combined with a cobalt blue with one extra dark factor before the visual violet materializes. Because this factor is dominant, no bird can be split for violet. Any bird with violet in its make up shows this by an alteration in its colour (e.g. violet dark green).

The following table shows how the violet character is inherited.

(Vv = Single factor violet. VV = Double factor violet. vv = non-violet.)

Mating	Resulting Expectation
Vv × vv	50% single factor violet (Vv) 50% non-violet (vv)
Vv × Vv	25% double factor violet (VV) 50% single factor violet (Vv) 25% non-violet (vv)
Vv × VV	50% single factor violet (Vv) 50% double factor violet (VV)
VV × vv VV × VV	100% single factor violet (Vv) 100% double factor violet (VV)

The visual violet is produced by pairing a bird from the blue series carrying the dark factor, that is cobalt or mauve, to a skyblue with a double factor for violet. Other pairings are a double factor cobalt to a normal skyblue, the resulting expectation being 25 per cent normal skyblue, 25 per cent cobalt, 25 per cent violet skyblue and 25 per cent violet cobalts. Half of the chicks can therefore be visually violet.

It should be remembered that violet to violet pairing does not give 100 per cent visual violets. This pairing will result in skyblues, single and double factored skyblues, cobalts and double factored cobalts, violets, mauves, and single and double factored mauves. In any event the quality of both visual violets is unlikely to justify such a pairing.

Grey

In the normal grey we have a bird of great beauty. It is a most popular variety and has frequently taken top honours on the show bench and will continue to do so for many years. There are two forms of grey, the English grey and the Australian grey, though it is now accepted that the former variety is practically non-existent. The latter is a variety which is bred in many birdrooms today sometimes in quantity. Genetically the Australian grey is of interest since there are two kinds, one carrying a single factor for grey and the other carrying a double factor. A single factor grey mated to a non-grey will produce 50 per cent greys and 50 per cent non-greys, while if a double factor grey is similarly mated to a non-grey it will produce 100 per cent greys. In both cases the resulting greys will be single factored greys. It is important to remember that no bird can be split for the Australian grey factor. It is either visibly grey or it is non-grey, and therefore the factor is described as dominant.

Australian greys appear in three shades, light, medium and dark greys. The light greys do not, for some inexplicable reason, seem to win as well as the medium and dark greys. These shades correspond to the skyblue, cobalt and mauve colours of the blue series.

The rules which govern the grey inheritance factor are straightforward.

Mating	Resulting Expectation
Single factor grey × Normal (non-grey)	50% Single factor grey 50% Normal (non-grey)
Single factor grey × Single factor grey	25% Double factor grey 50% Single factor grey 25% Normal (non-grey)
Double factor grey × Normal (non-grey)	100% Single factor grey
Double factor grey × Single factor grey	50% Single factor grey 50% Double factor grey
Double factor grey × Double factor grey	100% Double factor grey

It is impossible to tell visually in the Australian grey variety whether it is a single or double factored bird, the only test is to breed by examples 1 and 3 from the above chart.

When pairing it is preferable to mate medium greys to themselves or to dark greys, since both shades produced are then in contrast to the white face and frontal which is so attractive to the eye. The alternative if one wishes to build up a strain of greys and blues is to cross them periodically, the greys being invaluable for their ability to improve type in the blues though disadvantageously reducing the depth of colour in themselves. Some of the best greys have come from grey green/ blue × grey matings, the size and superior qualities of the grey green series improving the greys tremendously.

Grey greens
This variety, like the greys, blues and greens, is divided into light, medium and dark shades. Just as the light greys are not so desirable for showing, so also the light grey greens. The darker the depth of colour the better.

The distinguishing feature between the grey green and the olive is the cheek patch, the former being bluish grey while the latter is distinctly dark violet. The grey green has probably accounted for more major specials at open shows in the last thirty years than any other individual colour and the combination of grey greens with cinnamons is an ideal specialisation for any newcomer to the fancy who wants to win major awards.

Lutino
This plum eyed, deep buttercup coloured variety has a number of staunch supporters. Lutino is a form of albinism which is devoid of all colour pigment except yellow. There are two distinct kinds, the sex-linked and non-sex-linked, though the latter group are today uncommon and only held by specialist breeders.

It is the aim of every lutino breeder to reproduce birds with a deep buttercup yellow colour completely devoid of wing suffusion or greenish tinge on the body. These two latter faults are apt to creep in as a result of introducing non-lutino outcrosses in an endeavour to improve the type and head qualities. The best outcrosses have been light yellows but unfortunately these have to some degree declined in type of late.

In general therefore it is necessary to use an alternative variety to maintain colour and improve type. Grey yellows are sometimes available with the necessary requirements and grey greens are also a possibility, though these produce rather slow results when the out-crosses used are cocks. The outcross cock to a lutino hen produces split lutino cocks and non-lutino hens and therefore it is not until the split lutinos are used in the second generation that one can see any visible lutino results. A quicker way is to pair a lutino cock to an outcross hen; this gives lutino hens immediately in addition to split lutino cocks. Light green outcrosses can be used but care has to be taken to avoid the massive intrusion of green suffusion into the lutinos produced.

There is no objection to pairing lutinos where it is considered suitable. Only when size, type and colour starts to become faulty is it necessary to resort to the outcross methods.

There are today three main types of lutino fault to be seen on the show bench. The first are large birds with reasonable heads and good type but poor pale yellow colouring. Then there are smaller lutinos of poorer type but with fine deep buttercup coloured bodies. Lastly there are reasonable quality lutinos which have a green sheen on them plus a distinct suffusion or lacing effect on their wings. The yellow and buff theory (see page 59) must be applied to their breeding since it provides the necessary balance required.

Since lutinos are difficult to reproduce in numbers by comparison to other varieties, and because of the numerous coloration hazards referred to, the lutino is not for the beginner. I have only seen one lutino cock bird in nearly thirty years that had a head of width and size to equal the best light greens yet still possessed the perfect colour, and that bird regrettably never once reproduced.

The sex-linkage pairings for lutinos are the same as for cinnamons and opalines and can be checked against the sex linkage chart on pages 92–93.

Albino

As with the lutinos the prime object is to produce a bird devoid of any suffusion in the wings and without any indication of a blue tinge to the body. The feathering should be completely white.

When an outcross is required problems occur similar to those of the lutino, and most breeders use the normal grey. Albinos in the stud should preferably have the grey character in their background; should they have perhaps a blue line background, this would result in the blue suffusion being brought out in the albino chicks. Albino greys are the best albinos to use for the show bench and since it is relatively easy to obtain a high class normal grey, their type can easily pass to the albino progeny. Some breeders have had initial first generation success with the use of cinnamon greys as outcrosses but once the cinnamon tinge appears in the wings of the albinos it can ruin the complete line.

Yellow (black eyed)

There are light yellows, dark yellows and olive yellows to be seen on exhibition and there have been serious attempts to improve these attractive birds. The exhibition light yellow bird should be free of dark markings and green suffusion, the bird being clear yellow throughout. There are many light yellows shown today with heavy green suffusion and dark markings which are referred to as 'yellows of deep suffusion'.

Mating light yellow to light yellow is to be preferred, to maintain purity of colour, but is not always practicable. Breeders are apt to choose the best light green cock available from the point of view of type, but immediately the progeny become light green/yellows. The next season these split yellows can be reintroduced to the light yellows, choosing the palest of the splits where possible. The result will be a percentage of light yellows carrying the undesirable green suffusion and this is where the skill of the yellow breeder is put to the test in gradually working out that suffusion at the same time maintaining the head qualities and type required. A lutino strain, particularly if a buff good headed bird were available, even if of poor colour itself, would be well worth introducing to a strain of yellows. A further alternative is the grey yellows, which are the product of two colours, grey and yellow.

Opaline

Of the many beautiful and successful varieties which consistently win on the show bench none has been more popular than the opaline. Being one of the sex-linked characteristics, this feature can be allied to any colour you wish, but there are clear requirements in the standard laid down by the Budgerigar Society. These clearly state:

1. Mask extending over the back of the head and merging into general body colour at a point level with the butt of the wings where undulations should cease, leaving a clear 'V' effect between top of wings.
2. Wings to be opalescent and of the same colour as the body – markings should be normal and symmetrical.
3. Tail feathers not to be lighter than the mantle (i.e. the 'V' area is termed the mantle or saddle).

Nearly every aviary has a percentage of opalines amongst its stock.

This has arisen because their show features are in general superior to many other varieties. A number of opalines in each establishment may carry good quality top ends with an acceptable depth of mask and big spots, all features of great use to the breeder and exhibitor.

Against them there are several drawbacks, not least of which is the fault of head flecking. This is a bad feature, where a percentage of black markings appear in the frontal area and crown of the head; it is a severe handicap on the show bench. Often the bird with head flecking is also the possessor of a first class head as regards size and width, which tempts the breeder to use it for reproduction. Unfortunately this flecking is an hereditary feature, but to a limited extent it can be overcome by pairing the affected bird to a normal line known to be clean in this respect. The subsequent chicks may be perfectly clean or with luck only partially affected but such a pairing should only be employed with an exceptionally good headed flecked bird. Many breeders will completely disagree with this and say it is far better to eradicate the problem immediately and never use such a bird, so that there is no chance of subsequent flecking arising in later generations. Flecking can occur with any bird, but it happens to be more prevalent in opalines than any other and most cases in other varieties can be traced back to the use of opalines.

Another problem with opalines is the difficulty the breeder has in obtaining a clear mantle while at the same time acquiring normal wings. So many opalines have achieved the desirable mantle, only to display large clear patches of the body colour just below the wing butts. Conversely when the wings are correct it is the mantle which becomes suffused with black.

There are many successful studs that are 100 per cent opaline and always use opaline × opaline pairings. These studs continue to do well but they have ensured that the desirable opaline features have been fixed for many years before reaching this stage of specialization. If one is not careful continuous opaline to opaline pairings will result in the mask gradually shortening.

Opalines are sex-linked; pairings and their subsequent expectations can be checked against the sex-linkage chart on pages 92–93, substituting opaline for cinnamon.

Cinnamon and cinnamon opaline

In recent years the quality of the cinnamons that have appeared at open shows has been little short of phenomenal. Regarded by many as the most handsome of all the varieties, and being a sex-linked characteristic into the bargain, many beautiful combinations of cinnamon are seen. Cinnamon grey greens are generally the superior colour, their size winning over the cinnamon blue series. The best pairing is cinnamon to cinnamon if the partners are suited.

Allied to the cinnamons is another very successful, attractive variety, the cinnamon opaline. The combination of these two sex-linked features has often arisen because the breeder wishes to combine the fine quality feathering of the cinnamons with the coarser feathering of the opalines. In turn the large spots of the latter balance and improve the generally weaker spots of the cinnamons.

One word of warning – take care when pairing normals with cinnamons, cinnamon opalines and opalines, otherwise there will not be a pure bred grey, grey green, light grey or blue on the premises. Take care also when purchasing to improve a pure normal line since so many cocks are split for these sex-linked features.

Clearwings

Clearwings are composed of two groups, whitewings in the blue series and yellow-wings in the green series; they do not constitute a separate group of their own. There exists a separate society concerned with breeding this beautiful variety, the Clearwing Budgerigar Breeders' Association. The object of the clearwing breeder is to maintain without suffusion a clear white or yellow (as near buttercup as possible) in the wings, simultaneously with good depth of body colour to contrast completely with the wings. While achieving this balance efforts must continually be made to produce the ideal birds.

Most clearwing breeders pair whitewings to yellow-wings, resulting in yellow-wing/whitewing. Alternatively, in an attempt to improve head qualities, yellows and whites are paired to whitewings and yellow-wings respectively. It is essential these yellows and whites, in addition to their superior head qualities, have wing markings as faint as possible. There are numerous other pairings that may be considered by the enthusiast and much information is available through the C.B.B.A., membership of which is to be recommended.

Greywing

This variety has of late become less common on the bench. This is partially due to the fact that they are usually pitted against the cinnamons in the same class, where they are in most cases beaten fairly easily. However the greywing has greatly improved since the war and the fact that the characteristic is recessive has resulted in some excellent specimens occurring from time to time. At present there is not a greywing specialist breeder of note and until they are alloted separate classes it is doubtful if anyone will deliberately produce them. The danger to the conventional breeder is that once introduced, the greywing recessive character can be distributed throughout the stud in a very short time. Nevertheless this very attractive variety will continue to be admired, particularly the greywing green and greywing blue varieties in their respective shades.

Fallow

This non-sex-linked, red eyed variety with brown markings has never achieved any popularity and as a variety on the show bench is not to be considered by the serious exhibitor. It can be bred with any of the normal varieties, including the yellows and whites, or introduced as an alternative to greywings.

Yellow-face

There are two types of yellow-face, those the colour of which is confined to the face and others that have the colour spilling down over the breast. The latter is a fault. The yellow-face is not a popular variety but if allied to the normal grey, some excellent specimens can be produced. Normal greys of quality can usually be obtained and as the first outcross it is desirable to obtain the best yellow-face grey, with as much width and absence of neck, as possible. Lack of width and an excessively necky appearance seems to predominate with this variety, the birds with the necessary width and substance often having the chest spilling fault. While yellow-faced greys are most favoured, there are occasionally good specimens to be seen in cobalts and skyblues. It is important to retain the yellow face with the white faced series since if combined with the natural yellow faces of the green series it becomes masked and tracing the true yellow factor becomes impossible.

Yellow-faces can be either single or double factored; this can only be ascertained by breeding. If a yellow-face is paired to any blue series bird and results in all yellow-faced progeny, then the bird is a double factored yellow-face. If non-yellow-faced birds appear then it is a single factored bird.

Dominant and recessive pieds

We now come to two groups of budgerigar possessing broken coloration and known collectively as pieds. They are divided into two groups genetically and visually, called dominant pieds and recessive pieds. The dominant pied has become very popular as an exhibit over the past decade.

To differentiate whether a pied is a dominant or a recessive, examine the eye. All dominants have a normal eye, that is a black pupil surrounded by a white iris. Recessive pieds have a deep solid dark eye so there should be no trouble distinguishing the two groups. If a dominant pied is paired, for example, to a normal light green, the resulting progeny will either be light greens or pieds; the light greens produced will be pure as far as the pied factor is concerned (i.e. non-pied). Here lies their attraction to the serious exhibitor. He can pair his pieds to his conventional varieties without any fear of his resulting normal birds finishing up as split for pied and any non-pied produced from normal to pied pairings can be filtered back to the normals the following season. Recessive pieds paired with normals on the other hand give 100 per cent splits. When these splits are mated back to other recessive pieds the following year 50 per cent splits and 50 per cent recessive pieds are produced. Breeders of recessive pieds are therefore mainly specialists in pieds alone and have no worries about an aviary full of split pieds and pieds.

Dominant pieds are themselves sub-divided into two main groups at exhibitions, namely dominants and clearflights; of the former group the banded pied is very much sought after. The ideal band in the region of the stomach requires that it should be full and reaching in an unbroken band from side to side. Some have only a partial band but nevertheless can still be exhibited as banded pieds. A vital show point in dominant pieds is that each shall possess six spots as in the normals. Unfortunately many dominants moult out with less than that number and this fault has to be quickly eradicated in a stud if show specimens are going to be bred without this marring feature. Recessives are not required to have spots.

At present the dominant pieds have improved to the extent that little separates them from the best in the normal series, but it should be remembered by the breeder who keeps the conventional colours that introducing a dominant pied may reduce the quality, with regard to head and type, of the existing stud unless he is careful. This of course depends on the quality of the dominant pied that is introduced. Many breeders of dominants are against pairing of pied to pied. They argue that this pairing reduces size in the progeny and claim that non-pied to pied pairing gives superior results. Some also claim that the use of opalines and cinnamons is to be deprecated, but some of the best looking birds are opaline light green pieds.

To deliberately breed banded pieds is difficult, but they seem to turn up with the second generation once a banded has been introduced.

The use of the word clearflight can be very confusing as many dominant pieds have flights that are basically clear of markings. The standard states that the clearflight must possess seven flights completely free from markings and furthermore the tail should be similarly clear. Any markings whatsoever constitute faults. Some of the best results have come from pairing reasonably well marked cocks to hens that show just the head patch, the male progeny often being perfect clearflights.

A word of warning. I strongly advise breeders not to pair dominant pieds to recessive pieds or to birds known to be 'split' for the recessive character. This pairing can only result in the production of inferior, poorly marked specimens.

When breeding recessive pieds, there is likewise nothing to be gained by mating them together. The only way to improve their quality is to pair them to high quality splits which have resulted from first class normals. One must always endeavour to keep the recessive coloration as bright as possible and therefore the use of blues and light greens is advisable. Using greys as outcrosses can only dull matters.

Lastly there is the group known as dark-eyed clears. These result from the pairing of clearflights to recessive pieds. As yet this group is in its infancy and outstanding specimens have not yet been seen on the show bench.

9. Practical Breeding

The Breeding Season

Newcomers to budgerigar breeding will soon realize that any year is divided into three parts. From December to June breeding is in progress, depending when one starts; the following three months are devoted to training, and from August onwards the major exhibitions take place. There are roughly seven months devoted to reproducing and improving our stock and this period is of paramount importance to each breeder. If things go wrong in the breeding season then blame yourself. If you do so, and act to eliminate your management or design faults, then success will be your reward.

Controlled breeding

This book is directed towards producing the near-perfect bird which will ultimately win on the showbench and bring demand, from others, for the sale of the bird itself or for its progeny. The only way that this can be achieved is by controlled breeding of individual pairs in separate cages, allowing accurate recording of any chicks produced. These chicks can then be kept for subsequent pairing to relatives, or to birds bought from other studs.

The alternative system is known as colony breeding, where a given number of pairs are put into a flight along with an equivalent or greater number of nesting boxes and the birds are free to choose their own partners. This haphazard system is not to be recommended to the serious breeder.

Factors influencing breeding condition

Most studs of birds in the northern hemisphere are in breeding condition in November and early December and then decline until they are at their lowest in late January. Thereafter another upward phase occurs until a period in about early March when they are again at a peak. This however is a generalization and the fancier must use his own initiative in judging when to pair his birds, from their apparent condition at any one time. In the wild, budgerigars will not breed until there is sufficient food and water in evidence. Should those not be available, breeding will be withheld naturally for months or perhaps, in the extreme, for a year or so. However, when rain comes and grasses grow rapidly, instinct tells them to begin reproducing without delay.

Under artificial conditions in the aviary, where food and water are plentiful, this influence does not apply and the regular high and low peak condition periods are due to other factors. The hours of daylight are the main influence in the northern hemisphere and often, unknowingly, fanciers interfere with this natural cycle by providing too many hours of artificial daylight. Early closure of your stud in the evening is vital throughout the year, allowing the natural increase of daylight at dawn from the winter months onwards to control the environment. If you keep your stud awake until after 10.00 p.m., you can guarantee very mixed results; a 7.30 p.m. closure is ideal throughout the year.

When to start

The identification of breeding condition is not difficult, but is important if successful results are to be obtained. The cock in peak condition is bright eyed, tight in feather with an iridescent blue cere, and flies vigorously from perch to perch, hitting each with a bang as he alights. The hens are similarly active, with a rich nut brown cere; they call to the cock birds, especially early in the morning, and spend their non-eating periods chewing anything they can lay their beaks to. In contrast, the sexes out of condition are perhaps in a moult (though not always so), lethargic, dull eyed, with dull blue or even white-blue ceres in the cocks and white or whitish brown ceres in the hens.

Having considered the condition of your birds, one other factor, the show season, regrettably influences when you start breeding. The show season runs from August onwards, with additional young stock shows in June and July, though these have a limited value to the champions. If you start breeding in February, when your results overall will be better because of the milder and longer days ahead, then your young birds will be at least two months behind those reared by other fanciers who started in December. Budgerigar Society closed coded rings are issued on 1st January and many top breeders start one month before this so that their early chicks are ready to be ringed on that date. Many breeders put the starting date before their birds come into condition with disastrous results; it is best for the newcomer to learn the easy way – start in February or March, pair each bird according to its breeding fitness and then some of the problems associated with breeding will be avoided.

Maturity

When thinking in terms of breeding, consider whether your stock is sufficiently mature to reproduce and undergo the strain of rearing two full rounds of champion-sized pedigree chicks. There are varying opinions on the precise ages involved; it is possible to obtain chicks successfully from nine months old hens, but foster parents should always be allowed to do the rearing. The young hen must be given sufficient time for the ovaries to develop to maturity. The majority of fanciers agree that the minimum breeding age for a hen should be eleven to twelve months, with the cock a month younger. Budgerigars give their best in their second and third years, after which they decline somewhat; the fourth year is the limit for top class results in a breeding hen and perhaps the sixth year in the case of the cock. In practice, unless there is a particular reason to hold on to a bird it is rarely kept more than three seasons by champion breeders.

Preparations before pairing

In the weeks before you expect to pair up the first birds, ensure that the whole aviary is thoroughly cleaned; wash down with disinfectant and give a new coat of leadless paint. Scrub all the square cage perches, position nest boxes and bolt them into place. Update record cards and master book to deal with the new season. Change the bulbs in the dimmer circuit to ensure against failure and check the thermostats and heaters.

On the day before pairing, systematically check that every nest box has a handful of non-toxic sawdust in the concave and that every box is open and accessible to the breeding pair. Provide each cage with cuttlefish, an iodine block, a fresh bowl of grit, an open water receptacle and a large flat based bowl of the correct breeding seed mixture. The only additional item is a millet spray positioned near the nest box hole to encourage the hen in that direction, since it is she who is placed in the breeding cage first. Breeding birds should have large enamel receptacles for seed to ensure that, during the course of the day, at no time is there risk of the food running out before you can attend to it. Should the food supply run out, and remember the amount consumed increases considerably as the chicks grow, the parents become unstable, the rate of feeding drops and they have been known to desert altogether. Drinkers should also be large for the same reason. Those of the plastic fount type, which are clipped to the front of the cage are excellent for the small breeder providing he cleans them regularly every day. The tubes and bases become quickly fouled and coated with a transparent slime which if neglected can sour the water, and the birds themselves are then subject to contamination, resulting in poor feeding and enteric problems. Alternatively 3-in. diameter pottery vessels are easy to clean and refill daily. As with the feeding dishes, make sure the total quantity of water available is more than can possibly be consumed in one day.

Pairing

Having established which pairs are in full condition and satisfied yourself that each pair has, as far as you can tell, every chance of reproducing youngsters better than the parents, you are now set to start your season.

There are varying schools of thought on which of the sexes should be introduced to the breeding cage first. Some breeders prefer to have the nest box open from the start, others like it shut off for two days while the pair adjusts. It is largely a question of preference; not all the practices employed by one successful breeder will suit another establishment, so by all means try another method if one fails. The following routine is known to be successful and makes a good starting point.

On the first day, put all the hens in the breeding cages before 10.00 a.m., with the nesting boxes open. Often you will see that the hens, particularly maiden hens, are unsteady; the square perches under their feet feel strange and the sudden change from the spacious flight to a restricting compartment contribute to this. Leave them strictly alone until the following day, by which time they will have completely investigated their new domain, including the dark interior of the nesting box, and will know where the food and water are positioned. The following morning put in the cocks, which are mentally more stable and less excitable than the hens. Since they have become used to their surroundings, the hens devote all their attention to the new arrivals and older, more mature hens that have been through it all before are in the mating position within a minute. The cock birds, being more stable, couldn't care less where they are; the fact that a female in full condition and ready for mating is suddenly presented to them is more than enough compensation for the strange surroundings. There follows a brief courtship or display in which the pair dance along the perches and rap their beaks together hard and frequently. The hen in general stays on the one perch while the cock dives across to the other and back again several times. The adrenalin brings about a change, the most noticeable being the dilation of the pupils, which appear nearly white with a pin-point iris. The hen then lies across the perch and raises her tail, at which point the cock, facing the same direction, climbs on her back and swings his tail down underneath hers, at the same time extending one wing to help him hold on. He then presses his vent against that of the hen and with a treading and swinging motion quickly brings about a climax. Often the highly fit bird will return and repeat this within a minute. At the climax of mating the cock releases a quantity of seminal fluid containing large numbers of sperm. This fluid is mixed with the equivalent fluid produced by the hen. On contact the sperm swim up the oviducts of the hen and so fertilize any egg(s) which may be descending. Each egg is fertilized separately in most cases, but fertilization of a whole clutch at one go does occur sometimes.

Failure to pair

It used to be accepted to wait and observe mating take place; once this had happened the pair were allowed to continue alone. If you did not see the mating take place you were recommended to split them and try again later, or pair with other birds. Most breeders do not now worry about observing a pair mate. Birds are different in character, in the same way as animals. Some are vigorous and bold, others shy and retiring, so even if you do not see an immediate mating, just leave them alone and go out of the birdroom for the rest of the day. Many of the pairs which have provided full rounds have never been seen to mate. Birds are most highly sexed at 7 a.m. and this is the time when most mating is carried out. A positive guide to a failure to pair is to check the neat pile of sawdust you put in the nest box. If that has been undisturbed for two or three days you can be sure the pair is out of condition or immature, so you may as well divide them and try later.

Laying

In the next few days the hen will be seen going in and out of the nest box, spending longer in there each day. She will chew the box and it is a good idea for this reason to put a softwood block just under the entrance hole yet well away from the concave. She will then chew this in preference to the expensive box and it gives her something to do while incubating her eggs. At about the fourth day the droppings of the hen will be larger and on each succeeding day they increase still more and become copious. The first egg is usually laid seven to ten days after pairing, though allow up to eighteen days to elapse before deciding to break a pair up if there are no results. Some pairs will try to throw out all the sawdust you have put in initially, so replace this to ensure you have a good cushion by the time the first egg is laid. After the first, eggs are laid on alternate days until the clutch is complete. An average nest would consist of six eggs but odd pairs from time to time lay as many as eighteen, all fertile, though this has always been the result of fostering out their early eggs to other pairs.

Incubation

The period of incubation lasts eighteen days but allow an extra two days, since the hens do not always sit immediately on the first egg, only starting incubation with the laying of the second. The hen does all the incubating, the cock acting as protector and provider. By the time the third egg is laid it is possible, by holding the first egg against a strong light, to confirm fertility or otherwise. An area of red streaks to be seen covering the surface of one side of the yolk is the developing embryo. If this is not there once it is known the egg has been incubated for a minimum of five days, it can be assumed it is infertile. Do not handle the clutch at all once fertility has been established in one egg. This can only result in addled eggs and dead-in-shell chicks.

Hatching

After eighteen days of incubation, the egg hatches, though the actual process of the chick breaking through begins some thirty-six hours beforehand. A fine crack will be apparent at sixteen and a half days and this is increased slightly by the seventeenth day. The chick can also be heard squeaking as early as this and many fanciers are tempted to start 'helping' the chick out, thinking that the bird is struggling and overdue. This premature action finds the chick white in body colour with the yolk case still attached to the stomach, not fully absorbed; the death of the chick is certain within hours. The way in which any chick emerges from its shell is one of nature's wonders since there is no control by the parent other than incubation. The chick during its development grows a small white horn on top of its upper mandible and by rapping its head, within the confines of the shell, against the surrounding membrane and shell, rotating periodically as it does so, it gradually cracks and weakens the shell all round. Provided there are no problems the egg eventually breaks and hatching is completed.

The eggs were laid on alternate days and hatch in the same order, the last chick in a nest of six eggs being twelve days younger than the first.

Feeding the chicks

The chicks are fed primarily by the hen, especially in the initial stages of development. The cock sometimes assists but more usually feeds the hen to save her leaving the nest. The method of feeding is by regurgita-

17 (left) A show quality lutino cock, with perfect colouring.

18 (above) A champion lutino cock, showing frontal feathering over the beak.

Light green cock exhibiting width
d depth of mask.

20 Opaline grey green hen with the essential exhibition appearance of looking down.

21 An opaline cinnamon light green cock; a good square faced bird, marred only by eye flecking and a divided mask.

22 An opaline light green cock; a deep masked cock which should have greater width between the eyes and rounder spots.

23 An opaline grey cock, lacking in head quality.

24 An opaline grey green hen; an excellent hen but the superfluous spots must be removed before showing.

tion, the seed being eaten and swallowed by the adult, ground down to small particles in the gizzard, mixed with crop milk and brought up again and pumped into the chick(s). The quality of the crop milk is of paramount importance, the chick's growth rate being dependent upon it. Successful feeding of the chick from the moment of hatching is vital, though it is important to note that the parents will not feed a chick that is quiet. A red-bodied, lusty chick is what is required, the parent pushing the chick on to its back and regurgitating the necessary food into it. Instinctively the parents know what grade of food to give, depending on the size of the chick they are feeding. Pure fine grained crop milk is fed to the newly hatched, while those much older get almost whole grains.

Transferring
For a variety of reasons both eggs and chicks have to be transferred from nest to nest during the course of each season. It may happen you have some nests with eight to twelve fertile eggs. Obviously many chicks will be lost as they hatch, so it is advisable to mark each egg with the nest number with an indelible felt pen (ensure it has no smell) and move some elsewhere, where perhaps a quantity of infertile eggs have occurred, discarding the latter. You cannot, without running a great risk, transfer eggs to an empty nest; they will be destroyed almost immediately by the foster pair. However, once the foster parents have one egg then they will accept any number.

In the same way chicks can be moved, concentrating those of a similar age together in groups of four or at the most five. You cannot introduce a chick, without risk, into the nest of a pair which has not yet hatched one of its own. The problems of transferring chicks of three weeks or more are considerable in contrast to those younger. For some reason the older chicks are detectable as strangers by the foster pair and may be attacked immediately, so listen for any trouble when a big chick has been moved. A good tip is to rub the foster nest box droppings all over the newcomer, so it smells identical to the rest of the nest.

One method of keeping track of unringed chicks is by moving a chick of known colour into a nest of a contrasting colour, leaving identification until the nest is feathered. Yet again, one can move cinnamon and lutino chicks, which are red eyed, to black eyed nests. Even though the eyes are sealed their colour can be detected from the moment of hatching. If you have to put an unringed chick, perhaps a grey, into a nest also containing greys you can mark the back of the chick with an indelible marker until it is old enough to be ringed.

Ringing

To ring a chick, wash and warm your hands and, holding the chick in your left hand, grip one leg between thumb and forefinger, supporting the chick at the same time. Then slip the ring over the three longest toes and slide it up the leg. The back toe is then trapped between the ring and leg; by taking a pointed matchstick and slipping it under the trapped toe this will be released and the process is complete.

Rings are supplied with your personal code number which you retain for as long as you remain with the Budgerigar Society. They are also stamped with the year of issue and are serialized from one up to whatever figure you require.

To facilitate matters still further the colour of the closed rings is changed each year and all the Area Societies follow suit. It then becomes an easy matter for the individual to spot his current year's birds and furthermore, when judging, there is a quick method of checking there are no adults mixed up with the current year birds in breeder classes.

One to six weeks

After ringing you will see the beginnings of feathering on the back of each chick. This gradually resolves itself to a thick down at about the fifteenth day and the experienced eye will gauge how healthy the chicks are by the density of this early feather growth. Crops should be distended throughout the whole period if the parents are behaving normally, though do not be too worried if in the early morning some crops are found to be less than full. This is quite normal and once the adults get into their stride all will be well. From the down stage, the feathers lengthen very quickly and one can tell by the twentieth day exactly what colour the chicks are going to be. Body and feathers grow rapidly until at five weeks we have a nest of fully formed budgerigars which we term barheads. Instead of having a clear forehead, as in the mature normal bird, the chick at five weeks has feathers with bars across this area and these do not disappear until the first moult.

Leaving the nest

An awkward time arises when the chicks are five weeks old. The adult pair now starts to lay the second round with the fully grown chicks still in the nest box. Naturally these eggs will be kicked around and damaged unless precautions are taken (see page 113). Coinciding with this, the pair, particularly the hen, sometimes force out the grown chicks on to the cage floor where they shuffle around for a day calling for food. They eventually become bolder and venture to the perches, and later still

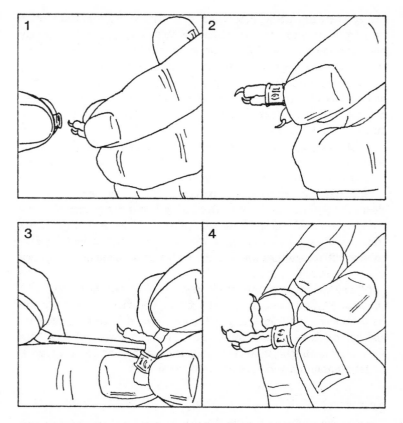

Ringing a chick

1. *Hold the chick in the left hand. With the first finger and thumb of this hand gather the three long toes together and gently hold them in position by the ball of the foot. Pick up the ring in the right hand with the first finger and thumb and slide it over the three long toes.*

2. *Place the ring over the ball of the foot.*

3. *Gently grasp the three long toes with the first finger and thumb of the right hand and at the same time take the ring between the first finger of the left hand. Gradually slide the ring up the leg as near to hock as possible. The short back toe is held by the ring against the leg. Insert a burnt matchstick between the toe and leg and gently prise the toe from the ring.*

4. *The ring is in position when the operation is complete.*

Reproduced by permission of the Budgerigar Society

realize where the nesting hole is and try to clamber back in. Once inside they are a nuisance, so keep removing them and induce them to stay out alongside the food dishes. You must now keep your eyes open on two points. The length of the tail will give you a good idea of the age of a chick at a glance. If it is not almost fully grown, you can be sure the chick is not old enough to be removed from the cage. You must also be sure that every chick is able to shuck seed for itself and has been able to do so for a few days.

Chicks are generally able to feed themselves one week after leaving the nest and therefore a total of ten days should be sufficient for them to have acquired the feeding technique.

Once satisfied remove the chicks concerned and as you do so check their rings against your records. Obtainable from any ring manufacturer are split celluloid rings. These are self or multicoloured rings with a split at one point; they are used to ring each complete nest for easy subsequent recognition when in the flights. With a ringing tool, they can be slipped on in seconds.

All chicks should go into stock cages for a while. Do not expect a six-week-old bird to adjust to a large flight. The chances are that it will be bewildered and frightened, will not eat even if it does see the food and will catch a chill as a result and contract enteritis. Put them into stock cages with food and a few adults to calm them and let them grow on for a minimum period of two to three months.

Number of nests

Fanciers aiming for top quality sized show material should keep to four chicks per nest and permit only two rounds of this number from each pair. Larger numbers will reduce the size of the chicks and the rate and quality of feather growth. A third round of eggs may be taken, but foster them elsewhere for rearing if you value your adults. They need a rest after months of feeding and many will have the added burden of the show bench later in the season. Should a pair be used purely as layers then four rounds may be taken if the hen will oblige but there is a risk that removal of as many eggs as this will discourage the hen and she could be ruined as breeding stock.

Heat and humidity

It must be arranged so that the temperature in your birdroom never falls below 45°F. If you are an early starter to the season heat is essential. You can breed without, and there will be a degree of success, but the problems will be magnified many times over, so the cost of installation will be insignificant when related to your total output at the end of the year. Black heat is preferable.

The dangers of low humidity in an aviary in this country are not as great as many fanciers believe. There should be a medium/high level of moisture in the air since under low moisture conditions the inner membrane, just beneath the shell of every egg, can become toughened with the result that the chick is unable to break through, becomes exhausted and dies. This is termed 'dead-in-shell'. However, 90 per cent of dead-in-shell birds are poor, weak chicks caused by bad feeding and not the toughened membrane. Low humidity is a cause but not the major one. If you feel that the atmosphere may be the slightest bit dry then dampen down the aviary with a sprayer. Some fanciers keep a few copper coins under the nest concave to retain dampness in the right place, but do not spray or dip eggs into water or you will lose more than you gain.

Termination of the second round
Once the second round chicks have left the nest the nest box should be closed or removed and the eggs remaining transferred if required or thrown away. Removal of the nesting site brings about cessation of breeding. Do ensure that your hens are returned to stock cages for a period to regain their strength to cope with the bigger flights. Stock hens beome very weak with breeding, so give them every consideration for the efforts they have put in.

Breeding Season Hazards

There is no such thing as the perfect season, only a good season in which your problems have been fewer than usual! If your management has been faultless then your problems will be minimized, but at any moment a problem may arise and the inexperienced breeder will be at a loss as to the right action to take. Remember that 'if things go wrong it's your fault' and attempt to be both perceptive and observant. Armed with the information given in this chapter you should be able to cope with any situation which might occur. When dealing with livestock one learns the hard way, so if you can avoid repetition of mistakes then your annual output will be that much better.

Infertility
The commonest complaint for poor breeding seasons is infertility.

There are so many possible causes of this that each must be considered by the fancier in turn.

1 Adult(s) out of condition.
2 Characteristically non-vigorous cocks.
3 Round smooth perches, instead of square.
4 Loose perches or swing perches.
5 Box-bound hens (i.e. hens which refuse to mate and stay in the nest box).
6 Coarse feathering around the vent.
7 Excessive artificial light resulting in tired birds.
8 Hereditary characteristics.
9 Pairing on the decline of the fitness cycle.
10 Deficiency of Vitamin E.
11 Lethargic stud – poor feeding.
12 Nervous, highly strung hens.
13 Immature parent(s).
14 Birdroom too quiet – cocks not stimulated by chatter from flights.

Addled eggs

An addled egg is one that has been fertilized but subsequently, at any stage during development, ceases to grow and dies. This condition can occur during the period from one to sixteen days and must not be confused with 'dead-in-shell', when the chick dies in the process of hatching. The causes of addling are numerous and these account for a large proportion of egg wastage every season; preventive action by the fancier can reduce these to a minimum.

I. CHILLING. If at any stage the incubating hen leaves the nest for longer than a few minutes the eggs will quickly chill and the embryo may die. Night disturbance by mice, flashing lights or sudden noise may be causes, alternatively the hen may be taken ill or simply go out of condition and move off the nest. Odd eggs are sometimes kicked to one side and second round eggs laid while first-round chicks are in evidence suffer badly in this manner. Temporarily transfer all such eggs to other pairs, replacing them as each nest is vacated by the fully grown chicks. Chilling is also frequently caused by the cold fingertips of the handler, who examines each egg for fertility as part of his routine. Once one egg has been confirmed fertile, leave the clutch alone as there is nothing to be gained by further examination.

2. DIRTY EGGS. Egg shells are porous and permit the interchange of gases and bacteria for the benefit of the developing chick. If coated with excreta eggs often become addled as a direct result of harmful bacteria entering the eggs; the sealing effect of the excreta also prevents the advantageous gaseous exchange.

3. WEAK EMBRYOS. Many studs suffer badly from lack of attention to high grade feeding, the barest minimum of cheap seed being offered. The effect of this is that the cocks produce weak sperm and the hens poor grade yolks, which are the unborn chicks' food source. The result, often put down to the fault of the birds themselves, is chicks dying at ten to seventeen days during incubation. Post-mortem examination will show white anaemic embryos, semi-formed and with barely any yolk left for continued development.

4. MISHANDLING. A very frequent cause of addling, not often realized, is careless handling of the eggs by the fancier. Every yolk is suspended within the egg by two fine gelatinous strands called chalazae. If the eggs are rotated quickly these strands break, allowing the yolks to descend to the lowest point, where they quickly addle. The parents rotate the clutch periodically to prevent addling. If the fancier picks up each egg and replaces it in a different position, he alters the continuity of the hen's egg rotation and addling results.

Dead-in-shell

This term is applied to any chick that started to break out of the egg but has died in the attempt. In 90 per cent of cases the reason is incorrect feeding, which results in weak embryos. These embryos have enough strength to start chipping, but no more and death within the shell is the result. The remaining percentage are either eggs that are chilled during emergence or eggs incubated in low humidity atmosphere. A very dry atmosphere has the effect of toughening the inner membrane of the egg through which the chick must break. Should this be excessively dry then the chick has insufficient strength to chip through it and quickly dies.

Punctured eggs

All hens should have their claws clipped before pairing to reduce the number of punctured eggs that will inevitably occur as they settle and drag the eggs under them during incubation. Any punctured eggs found may be discarded immediately, even if they have sealed themselves again, since they never hatch.

Soft shells

Some hens lay one egg in the course of a round that is like a soft balloon; the cause is malfunction of the shell gland. Hens that always lay soft eggs may be discarded since experiments to rectify the malfunction rarely meet with success.

Over- and under-sized eggs

Occasionally a hen lays one egg that is about double the normal size. They are sometimes double yolked, sometimes fertile, yet rarely hatch successfully. There are records of successful twins being born but usually one embryo dies and this infects the other, with fatal results.

Non-laying hens

From time to time a pair will mate in the usual way and a mature hen with all the signs of loose droppings and swollen vent area will not produce any eggs. These are termed non-laying or internal-laying hens and are useless.

Single egg layers

Certain hens, particularly highly bred pedigree hens, even though they are fully mature, drop only one egg per round. If of high quality it may be worthwhile using but there is a risk of producing further hens similarly affected. Transfer all such eggs immediately and allow the hen to lay another round.

Egg-eaters and ejectors

One parent sometimes develops the annoying habit of eating the eggs as they are laid. Remove the cock to establish which bird is at fault and should it be him then remove him each day an egg is due, transferring it to another nest as soon as it is laid. If it is the hen, a special concave has to be constructed with a $\frac{3}{4}$ in. hole in the centre to allow the eggs to drop through as they are laid, into a sawdust lined receptacle. Ensure there are no flat areas available for the hen to lay elsewhere – no matter where she lays, the egg must roll through the hole.

Parents that throw out eggs from the box can be dealt with in the same way.

Egg binding

Sometimes a hen, frequently a maiden hen, is unable to lay an egg which is mid-way between the shell gland and the vent. It is often the first egg that is involved, the cause being inability of the muscles in the vent area to relax and allow the egg to pass. Cold conditions are a contributory factor. The outward symptoms are characteristic, the hen being found in the nest box or on the floor of the cage with distended feathers, dilating pupils and a swollen vent. If light pressure is applied the egg can be felt quite easily. Remove the hen immediately to a source of heat, either a hospital cage or infra-red lamp, and lubricate the vent area with warm olive oil. This works in nearly every case, but if it does not then hold the vent area over a warm steam bath and all will be well within a few hours. Don't breed again with the hen for at least three months. Studs given diets containing cod liver oil do not as a rule suffer much with this complaint.

Box-bound hens

Certain hens will produce infertile clutches when paired to proven cocks and suspicion must immediately arise that they are staying within the confines of the nest box, emerging only to excrete. It usually means that the respective cock is on the quiet side sexually, so another vigorous, active male that chases the hen out of the box and mates immediately must be considered. This is the most direct and positive action, the original cock being mated to a hen known not to have this habit. Should an alternative cock not be available, the hen can be pushed out of the box for an hour each morning, as this is the period of highest sexual activity in most aviaries.

Assisting hatching

If the stud has been fed properly, so that the chicks are healthy and strong, it should not normally be necessary to help the chicks out of their shells. This interference is required occasionally in every stud but if your timing is slightly incorrect then the chick will be lost. The method used is to hold the egg with the cracked area uppermost and by using a sharpened matchstick describe a circle round the widest point of the egg, making sure that you cut through the inner membrane as well as the shell. A little blood will appear from the membrane and if the operation is correctly timed and performed the chick will be active and red bodied. If the chick is pale with a large amount of yolk attached to the stomach, you have opened it too soon and the chick will die. Assuming you have a suspect egg this is the sequence to follow having first checked that eighteen days have elapsed.

SOUND	APPEARANCE	ACTION
Quiet tapping	1/16 in. crack	Too soon—replace
Quiet tapping	Group of fine cracks	Too soon—replace
Quiet tapping	Cracks plus brown line	Too soon—replace
Weak squeaks	Cracks plus tiny hole	Too soon—replace
Medium squeaks	Cracks and early discoloration	Too soon—replace
Loud squeaks	Crack line round circumference—creamy patches, moist membrane	Normal hatching—replace
Loud squeaks	Crack line round circumference—creamy patches, dried membrane	Assist
Loud squeaks	Large hole—drying membrane	Assist

Remember, if it is the first chick to be assisted in the clutch, to leave the loose shell in situ, so that the hen accepts her first is hatching, otherwise she may kill it at once.

Crushed chicks
Some hens when incubating are tight-sitters, this is a tendency encouraged by ultra-cold conditions and results in day-old chicks becoming crushed and flattened. If you suspect this may happen substitute one with a five-day-old chick to lift the hen up and protect those yet to hatch. Do not be too hasty in assuming the hen is sitting tight, though, as often crushed chicks are those which are weak upon hatching, do not squeak and in consequence are not fed.

Unfed chicks
It is vital that a chick be fed within a few hours of hatching otherwise it will die or become a poor-doer. Should the first chick that hatches not be fed, you should immediately obtain a three-day-old chick that

has a bulging crop from elsewhere. This active little chap will often start the hen feeding, or the cock for that matter. Should this not succeed you can transfer, but if there is nowhere to transfer to you are left with only one solution. Mix a teaspoonful of Complan, which is obtainable from any chemist, with warm, boiled water and add some glucose. Lay the chick on its back where it will protest and squeak. Place a drop of the mixture over the beak and keep it there. Gradually the mixture will be swallowed and after a few minutes you will see the crop fill. Replace the chick under the hen and she will take over from there and start to feed.

With older chicks that are underfed, transferring must take place immediately.

Inflated crops
Chicks found with air-filled crops must be assisted by piercing the bag with a sterilized needle. The crop will return to normal but the process may have to be repeated daily for as long as necessary. If ignored the chick will waste and die.

Single chicks
If for one reason or another a single chick is being reared in a nest, do transfer it if at all possible, because there is a good chance that the hen will not feed a singleton very well. It needs a nest of three or four chicks to bring out the best in every pair, so transfer to meet this end.

Stunted chicks
A frequent occurrence in all studs is the nest with one or more chicks that have obviously fallen behind the others in growth rate and are stunted. In these the head looks excessively large and vulture-like, the legs are thin especially at the tops of the thighs, the crop has the minimum of food and the breastbone appears unduly sharp. These chicks are never likely to do well and your concern must be for the fittest. All such chicks should be put down as soon as they are noticed, since there is a danger that they will sour the adults during regurgitation, with subsequent disaster to the remaining fit chicks.

Rigid legs
Chicks found with their legs spreadeagled at right angles to their bodies and the joints seemingly fused and unable to bend are the result of close sitting by the hen on a shallow concave, with no sawdust or dry excreta beneath the chick to allow for the pressure. To prevent this, one infertile

egg should always be present when the remainder have hatched. Chicks found with the legs so displaced may be put down immediately as there is no chance of recovery.

Rickets – see page 166.

Sudden death of older chicks

One sometimes inspects a nest box of two- or three-week-old chicks and finds one dead with a full crop and no evidence of disease. Perhaps the next evening you find one or two more similarly dead in other nests and you are at a complete loss to know the cause. It could be your feeding that is at fault, so examine every item thoroughly, as the first step asking yourself whether there is a deficiency or excess of vitamins in any form, or perhaps any poisonous contamination? Next examine the floor of the nest box because older chicks begin to pick around the floor; something may be obvious or perhaps the sawdust you have used may be from a poisonous tree. Certainly if more than three or four chicks die without disease in a stud of say thirty pairs, you can look to your management; the cause must be more than the isolated heart attack.

Death of one parent

For a variety of reasons one of the adult pair may die suddenly leaving a number of awkward situations requiring quick decisions.

Cock dies leaving hen incubating
The hen can be left for a week quite safely and can certainly be allowed to hatch a few chicks if necessary. It is a risk to allow the hen to feed and rear four chicks on her own since she can desert at any time. Transfer at the egg stage as soon as possible.

Cock dies leaving hen with full nest of feathered chicks
This situation demands taking a chance and allowing the hen to complete the round. Do not shut off the nest box too soon otherwise, in her distress at not being able to lay again, she will not feed the chicks that surround her.

Hen dies leaving chilled eggs
Even if the eggs are discovered ice cold, do not despair. Warm them *slowly* in your hand, place them under another hen, allow an extra day for hatching and you may well be successul. Mate the cock to another hen.

Hen dies leaving cock to feed chicks

The solution to this depends on the age of the chicks. If they are un-feathered you must transfer, since the cock cannot be relied upon to cover the chicks for warmth. If the chicks are feathered, however, he is quite capable of finishing off the round but do give him a long rest upon completion.

Tired adults

A sure sign that the adults are tiring is the ceres changing colour. Sometimes the hen's cere may turn slowly white and the cock's by com-parison turns dark brown, almost black. They may have appeared in condition to start with but were probably on the downhill cycle when paired. Complete the round or transfer and return them to the flight.

Feather plucking

This is a nervous habit which makes one parent, frequently the hen, pluck the down or more mature feathers from the heads and bodies of the chicks. There are varying degrees of severity, from adults which merely take the fine down from the backs of the two-week-old chicks, stopping as the chicks grow older, to those who savagely strip the six-week chicks, taking the feathers and flesh from the head and wing butts and damaging them permanently. This must not be confused with the case of grown chicks that are attacked to expel them from the nest.

Most experts agree there is little that can be done to change this habit in an adult, and some believe it is hereditary. The guilty partner may be obvious because of bloodstains on the bib and one solution is removal of the adult concerned. An alternative, if the hen is guilty, is to allow the chicks to grow to three and a half weeks of age, and place an identical nest box on the floor of the cage with a quantity of the original nest box droppings on the concave. Put the affected youngsters there and the cock will in most cases feed them until they become self-sufficient. Most fanciers agree that there are perhaps four causes of feather pluck-ing, namely nervous reaction, boredom, protein deficiency or just plain cussedness; since the first and last are the most common reasons it is better worked out of the stud as soon as possible.

Attacking the chicks

Occasionally when a chick is about to leave the nest or is ailing, the hen will attack it to such an alarming degree that half of the skull may be destroyed leaving perhaps only one eye, the beak having been torn off in the process. The suffering chick must be quickly put down. When chicks leave the confines of the box the cock may carry out similar attacks, again often picking on one of the clutch, and feeding the remainder well in between finishing-off the poor unfortunate.

The causes are often difficult to establish in such cases, the attack on a sick bird and efforts to kill it being the only understandable reason. The cocks are often sexually frustrated when the chicks arrive in the cage and as a result endeavour to tread the chicks who obviously do not respond. This lack of response sometimes drives a cock to peck the back of a chick's head, drawing blood and killing it. Other cocks try to feed a chick on the cage floor, but the chick having dropped into a new environment does not seek the offered food and turns its back. The cock raps the chick on the back of the head, blood is drawn and the result is the same. In such cases, removal of the chick or preferably the offending parent is the only solution.

Foster pairs

Many fanciers use known top feeding pairs to foster eggs and chicks from birds of superior quality, the eggs of the foster pair being discarded. This is a very good practice to follow when you have bought a superb outcross and are anxious to obtain as many eggs as possible. By allowing a new outcross hen, for example, to lay at least two rounds of eggs, transferring these directly to foster pairs on completion of each clutch, you can acquire a larger number of progeny from your purchase than in the normal way. The hen can subsequently have a brief rest in the flight before mating to another cock. It is advisable to put two foster pairs down to breed with every major pair, to receive the first clutch of eggs, putting a further two foster pairs down two days after the transfer of the first clutch.

One cock to three hens

In cases where you have a particularly adaptable and vigorous cock bird of high quality try, in conjunction with a group of foster pairs, pairing him up to three hens at the same time. This is achieved by pairing him to the first hen, which we will call hen A, one morning. That evening he is placed with hen B and the morning after with hen C. The second evening he goes back to hen A and so on, the process being continued until all three hens have laid their clutches. It is possible to obtain over forty chicks from such a cock over a six- to seven-week period; this is achieved by using really reliable foster pairs, not maiden fosters. The advantage of this method is that the hens emerge from the boxes as soon as the cock is returned to them and mating takes place immediately.

The disadvantage is the extra work involved with foster pairs and moving the bird around continually. The rewards are great if you succeed, but it is essential you know the habits of your birds inside out and it is not a practice for the beginner to try.

French moult – see page 168

Mandibles – beak deformities
It is vital that throughout the period of growth from ten days to five weeks, the mandibles of every chick are inspected, particularly the upper mandible on the inside where it joins the fleshy part of the mouth. This point is the growing area *not* the tip of the beak. An accumulation of food particles, forming a cement-like pad at this point can occur, seen as a black patch. If this is not removed, the growth of the upper mandible ceases, allowing the lower mandible to gain in length. The result is an 'undershot beak' and the bird is permanently deformed. If you remove the pad every forty-eight hours, using a pointed matchstick, there will be no problem. Any similar accumulating food in the lower mandible must also be removed. 'Overshot beak', where the upper mandible grows to double its normal length, is normally confined to older pet birds not given the chance to wear down the beak on chewable surfaces. Efforts to rectify both forms of distortion by pruning back with nail clippers are sometimes successful and it is certainly worth trying, especially in the former case where the growth of the lower mandible must be held back until the upper attains its normal length.

Concaves
Every fancier becomes concerned towards the end of the first round when, due to the accumulation of excreta, the general level has been raised perhaps an inch or more and the eggs of the second round are not contained in any depression. The faeces are best removed and the level reduced when the first round youngsters are still within the box and the first egg of the second round has been laid. Do not remove quite everything. Leave in a handful of the old dirt mixed with fresh sawdust, so that the parents accustom themselves quickly to the change in level. To leave clean sawdust where there was none before would risk the parents losing interest in their chicks with the result that feeding would be minimal.

Deep litter
Every fancier will always try to keep his birdroom clean. The only

time in the season that you should depart from this is the breeding season, when cage trays should be left alone. This is the deep litter method. Every time they are withdrawn, not only are the birds in that box affected, but also those in the immediate vicinity. Each occasion there is the upheaval of removing all your utensils, drawing out the tray, scraping and returning each item, with the respective pairs taking a backward step in the rearing process. Even though this is not apparent immediately, it will manifest itself with smaller chicks than you would have under absolutely quiet conditions. All heavy droppings can be removed separately using a small trowel, leaving the major clean-up until the end of each round.

Visitors – disturbance

A ban on visitors in the first four months contributes to a reduced percentage of troubles and a general improvement in feeding. The ban must also be extended to members of the family and pets if you are to be consistent in your efforts and, while it may prove difficult, the results will more than compensate.

Smells

The sense of smell in budgerigars is acute and you must wash your hands before touching any nests. If you have patted the dog on the way and then handled some chicks, you stand a good chance of the parents deserting or even killing the chicks and throwing them out. Anything which changes the smell in a nest must be guarded against and it is even worthwhile, after washing, running your hands through the oil-impregnated seed since the birds are fully accustomed to its smell. When transferring chicks, particularly older chicks, rubbing their bodies in the droppings of the foster pair will often lead to the chick being accepted quite readily, whereas a strange smelling chick from next door would be quickly attacked.

Wet nests

If the floors of the nest boxes are coated with wet excreta this is the result of incorrect feeding. Ideal conditions give a humid box with the roof damp on the inside, sometimes slightly mouldy, yet with the floor covered with loose dry droppings none of which adhere to the feet of the chicks or parents. The odd wet nest, if it is the exception to the overall pattern, is normally caused by the metabolism of one parent being incorrect, this affecting the digestion of the chicks which then excrete wet droppings. Be careful when using sawdust to dry up such floors and do not put too much in at any one time.

Red mite – see page 163.

Nest inspection – starving cocks
As part of your daily routine it is vital that from the first day of pairing you inspect every nest box. Failure to do so from the start will result in not spotting the cock that has been feeding his hen but not himself and is beginning to starve. This is a frequent occurrence, many such cocks having an empty crop for perhaps only a few hours. Their condition is enough for them to be chilled, become ill with enteritis and of course in this state they stay in the nest box for warmth. If there is no daily inspection, then another dead bird is a certainty.

10. Training for Shows

The training of the birds that are to be exhibited is the hardest part of the season. The breeding and show procedures are relatively straightforward and you gradually improve these through acquired experience, but every year the hardest part is to steady the chicks sufficiently to enable them to relax and display their quality to advantage on the show bench.

Preparation begins in the nest box

The prelude to training is frequent handling of the chicks in the nest box from four weeks onwards, during which time they become used to the size and look of your hands. Provided you move slowly and deliberately at such times you will gain the confidence of each nest and because of this early attention they will be easier to deal with when introduced to show cages.

Parental influence

Many chicks reared by nervous, highly strung parents are similarly disposed and this is largely brought on by environmental conditions rather than hereditary factors. Chicks reared by such parents tend to squawk whenever the nest box is touched and when they emerge into the cage they fly madly about, banging themselves hard as they do so, whenever approached. Nervous parents should therefore be dispensed with for rearing.

Training flights

When removed from their parents, all youngsters should be introduced to stock cages, converted to training units by the introduction of show cages at certain points. Fanciers with sufficient room and finance to have a section, or even a separate birdroom, set aside for this purpose are lucky and such an area should be included in the 'ideal aviary'. The object from six weeks to four months is to accustom all your birds to a fairly restricted area, in a position where there is a reasonable amount of traffic passing. It is useless having these cages at one end of the aviary which you visit only occasionally. Far better to have them in the middle, where you and visitors congregate, so that the birds quickly become used to your presence.

It is also an advantage if they are fairly crowded, with some eighteen birds in a six foot cage. At the end of each of my own flight cages I have fitted a standard show cage and by hanging millet sprays on the bars each morning I induce the chicks to enter. They become used to the shortened perches of the show cage and also accept the change from square perches in the flight to round in the show cages quite readily. Completely ignore these first round youngsters while they are there for a period of six to eight weeks until shortly after they have moulted, when they are ready to put into the large flights to grow on and develop their wings.

The rough stage

At the beginning of the season, when the fully fledged chicks are in their boxes, you inspect each of them and pick out the good ones. Instinctively at this stage you are delighted with them. The moult then arrives and is completed and for a month immediately following, these early 'corkers' seem to have disappeared. This is the 'rough stage'. If you are able to take a holiday during this time you will find on your return that many birds will look as different again. Their weight is returning fast, the head widths and frontal bulges which were absent are now apparent and your early hopes start to materialize. Once they are through the rough stage it is time to withdraw individual birds for assessment and concentrated training for the shows ahead.

Selective group training

Having brought the select group back to the stock cages, they will be very fit and racy and for a few days will be difficult to calm. Their body weight, though improved by exercising, will still not be anywhere near the show weight and this has to be put on by moderate confinement and top quality feeding. Remember when a bird goes to a show it eats the barest minimum and loses weight very fast as a result, so you do no harm by feeding it extra well beforehand.

After a week or ten days start to give individual treatment to each bird, the very best being the first to get attention. The procedure is simple but time consuming since it has to be carried out each evening. Have four show cages, hanging in various places, into each of which go three, sometimes four, birds. As you put the birds in, remove any untidy broken body feathers particularly in the vent region, clean up the mask and generally go through the show preparation routine with each bird. Then leave them overnight, each with a millet spray opposite the perch, and return them to the cages the following morning. After several sessions in the show cages start chatting to them, keeping your hands out of sight. The caged youngsters respond well to being talked to and even nervous specimens will soon perch. However there are always some stubborn birds who seem to have forgotten all their early work, so individual treatment has to be meted out.

Refusal to perch

Some birds may refuse to perch and prefer to remain on the floor, more often than not endeavouring to bury their heads under the water pots. This can be very frustrating. The solutions to this are either to turn the show cage upside down, or if the bird persists in climbing the bars and chewing the show fronts, to insert a glass front or fix a celluloid sheet to the inside of the bars. In addition a heavy soaking in water will sober even the most unruly bird. If the bird is soaked in the early morning, several times during one week, and allowed to dry out in a *dry* show cage into which you have also put an 'old stager' who has not been sprayed, this rarely fails. Remember that horses have to be broken in and budgies are no different. Some unfortunately are more stubborn than most.

Use of the judging stick

When training is virtually completed the birds should be introduced to the chromium plated shiny judging sticks that are used at shows. Careful deliberate movements with the stick, inducing the birds back from the floor to the perches, will soon persuade calm youngsters into accepting the stick. Do not attempt to dig birds out of corners with the stick.

11. Exhibitions

The Budgerigar Society Show Rules

1. The colour feeding of Budgerigars is debarred; also the use of any preparation whatsoever which causes the birds in the slightest degree to show unnatural colour, or the specific use of agents for the sole purpose of promoting artificial growth. The trimming of wings and/or tail is also debarred and it is an offence to cut an official ring for the purpose of putting it on the leg of a Budgerigar and to exhibit a Budgerigar wearing more than one closed coded ring. The exhibition and sale of Budgerigars so treated is strictly forbidden and members showing or selling such birds render themselves liable to severe disciplinary action. Judges and/or any member of the Executive Committee, or any member of the General Council if there is not a member of the Executive Committee present, or the secretary of the show if there is neither a member of the Executive Committee nor of the General Council present, may impound any bird and the cage in which it was exhibited which they consider has been faked or dyed in any way, or is wearing an unrecognized ring in Breeders' classes or is presented in any fraudulent or misleading manner whatsoever. In all cases of alleged dyeing, even though tests may be made at the show, the bird must be impounded and forwarded to the General Secretary of The Budgerigar Society. The judge or judges and/or any member of the Executive Committee, or the General Council, or the secretary of the show will give the exhibitor and the General Secretary of The Budgerigar Society notice of impounding by personal intimation or telegram immediately, and by registered post within seven days thereof, specifying the alleged offence. The impounded bird shall be immediately forwarded to the General Secretary of The Budgerigar Society, it being insured for £100. The judge, judges, or the member of the Executive Committee, or of the General Council or the secretary of the show shall make a note in writing of the code number and serial number and year number from the bird's ring in the presence of witnesses to ensure identification. At the show and before the bird is actually impounded it shall be examined by the judges and/or members of the Executive Committee or General Council or the show secretary, who will forward their report to the Secretary of The Budgerigar Society, who will take any action necessary thereon in accordance with the Society's rules. The Society or any of the officials

concerned with the impounding of a bird will not be responsible for any loss sustained to the bird or otherwise during such impounding, and it shall remain impounded until such time as the investigations are complete and, if necessary, full disciplinary action taken.

1a. A judge's decision is final subject to show rule 1 but judges are instructed to consult other judges when in doubt regarding a particular exhibit before making a decision.

2. Special prizes offered by the Society shall only be competed for at Patronage Shows. Members must mark their entry forms 'B.S'. Failure to do so debars the exhibitors from taking any 'B.S.' award, with the exception of best in show.

3. PARTNERSHIPS – (a) Any member of the Society who enters into a partnership or arrangement with any other member or members must give notice in writing to the Secretary, stating the names of the parties concerned in the partnership, and entry forms to show secretaries must be correctly worded, clearly showing that such exhibits are the joint property of the exhibitors concerned. Members of any partnership must exhibit solely in the section of the highest-ranking member of the said partnership, and each member must be a paid-up member of the Society. In the case of partnerships formed between the end of a breeding season and the start of a show season, a certificate may be obtained on request to allow the new partnership to exhibit current year birds wearing rings bearing the code number of either partner in the breeders classes for the first year *only* of the partnership. In the event of a partnership dissolving, a certificate may be obtained on request, from the General Secretary, by either partner to enable them to show partnership ringed birds in the breeders classes under their own names for the remainder of the show season. Failure to observe these partnership regulations shall debar the allocation of all B.S. awards. (b) Where two or more exhibitors breed or keep their Budgerigars at one establishment, aviary or dwelling, such exhibitors must exhibit in the highest section of the said exhibitors. This rule also applies to Junior Members.

4. 28th February shall be deemed to end the exhibition year. Thus a bird hatched at any time during the current year can compete as a young bird up to 28th February in the following year. All exhibits competing in Breeders' classes must have been bred by and wear the official coded closed ring of the actual exhibitors. No nomination is required for ring scheme awards.

5. All entries made by members at shows supported by the Society which are too late for printing in the printed or duplicated catalogue will be debarred from taking any Society awards.

6. No exhibit shall be eligible for any Budgerigar Society Special Prize at any Patronage Show unless it is itself a first prize winner in its class at the show concerned, except in the class where the first prize winner is awarded best in show or best in section. In this class the second prize winner may compete for second best in show. If the winner of best in show is a certificate winner the runner-up for that certificate should also be considered for second best in show when such a special is scheduled. (Show promoting societies are strongly urged to adopt this rule for their own specials in order to make the judges' task easier with regard to the Budgerigar Section.)

7. At all shows receiving the patronage of The Budgerigar Society exhibitors understand and agree that the managements and/or any member of the Executive Committee present at the show concerned is empowered to handle and examine exhibits in the Breeders' classes if considered necessary.

8. The counting of points for Budgerigar Society special prizes at Patronage Shows shall be as follows: The seven highest awards in each class to count for points, first to count seven points. If less than seven exhibits, the first award shall count the same number of points as there are exhibits in the class. Each award after the first to count one point less than the award next above.

9. All exhibits must be shown in the standard show cage with the white ivorine plate on the front rail and no markings or labels other than the class label shall appear on the show cage front rail. The class label shall be centred on the front rail.

10. Floor of cages to be covered with any seed suitable for Budgerigars but millet sprays – whole or in part – shall not be permitted until after judging.

11. Judges officiating at shows held under the rules of the B.S. shall not be allowed to exhibit in the Budgerigar section.

12. DEFINITION OF JUNIOR, BEGINNER, NOVICE AND INTERMEDIATE. *Junior* – A junior paying a juvenile subscription must exhibit in junior classes only but the best junior bird should be judged along with other birds for the best in show. In the case of championship shows it must first compete for best of its colour.

Beginner – A beginner may exhibit in beginners' classes for three show seasons, as from the 1976–77 show seasons, or until he or she has won four first prizes in beginner section in full classes in competition at open shows, whichever is the longer period.

Novice – A novice may exhibit in novice classes for three show seasons, or until he or she has won four first prizes in novice section in full classes in competition at open shows, whichever is the longer period.

Intermediate – An intermediate may exhibit in intermediate classes for four show seasons, or until he or she has won six first prizes in intermediate section in full classes in competition at open shows, whichever is the longer period.

Note I – A full class shall be seven exhibits with not less than three exhibitors.

Note II – A member who commences the season as a beginner, a novice or an intermediate may continue as such until the end of that show season, even if he or she has attained a higher status.

Note III – Breeders' classes and any age classes at open shows are considered 'OPEN' competition for the purpose of the above definitions.

Note IV – In the case of more than one member residing at the same address they shall each take the same status as the other, that being the highest status of any one of them. For example: if one is an intermediate and the other a novice, they must both show as intermediates. This condition does not apply to unrelated sub-tenants. Where two or more exhibitors breed or keep their budgerigars at one establishment, aviary, or dwelling, such exhibitors must exhibit in the highest section of the said exhibitors.

Note V – If a bird wins a first in a class containing fewer than seven exhibits and not less than three exhibitors but then wins Best in Section, the win counts as first prize in the application of wins conditions in the above definitions. (That such wins shall not count towards status unless there are not fewer than six exhibitors in the section.)

Note VI – The status conditions commence from the first year a member exhibits. No allowance will be made for a break in continuity of exhibiting.

13. Any exhibitor may, if he or she desires, exhibit in a section higher than that of their present status, but having once done so (irrespective of not having been awarded a prize in the higher section) shall not be allowed to exhibit in a lower section at any future show, except that, in the case of intermediate or beginner exhibitors, at shows where no intermediate or beginner classes are scheduled, they may enter in the next higher section without losing their lower status. An exhibitor is not allowed to exhibit in more than one Budgerigar section.

Note I – Birds kept at the residence of a person who has exhibited in a certain status cannot be shown by a new owner in a lower status.

14. No person under suspension shall be allowed to judge or exhibit at any show held under the rules of the Budgerigar Society.

15. All exhibits must be the sole bona fide property of the exhibitor.

16. A bird must not be exhibited under the person from whom it was purchased, nor under the breeder and that a bird which has been bought must not be exhibited until it has been the property of the purchaser and in his keeping for not less than twenty-eight days.

17. RE-JOINING MEMBERS. Any person who has been completely out of the Fancy, and who has not owned nor exhibited birds for a period of five years, on re-joining the B.S. can take one status lower than that he had enjoyed when he was previously a member of the B.S.

18. Members re-joining the Society can be issued with their old code numbers providing they are available and all back subscriptions paid up. The paying of back subscriptions does not, however, entitle members to qualify for the ten years unbroken membership in connection with the judges' panel.

Widows of members who wish to do so can apply for membership and have their husband's code number but they must also take his exhibitor status.

19. CHAMPIONSHIP SHOWS (Procedure). A judge will judge the best of his/her colour, which will go forward for the award of best in show. The best in show will be selected from the best bird of the thirteen colours (which will include the best junior bird if it has been judged best of its colour). After best in show has been judged, it will be necessary to ensure that the proposed certificate winners are wearing an official ring. If a bird judged the winner of a certificate is found to belong to a non-member of the B.S., or not nominated B.S., the bird second in class should be considered for the award together with the next best in colour. Then the remainder of the specials will be judged and, finally, ring numbers of certificate winners must be checked and inserted on the certificate by the judge immediately on completion of all judging before he signs the certificate. Once a bird has been given an award of best in its colour it cannot thereafter be beaten by a bird of its colour for any other B.S. award.

The Budgerigar Society Standard Show Cage

Incorporating Patent No. 755106

Specification

SIZE: Overall measurements: 14 in. long, 12 in. high, 6½ in. wide.

WOOD: Top and bottom, ¼ in. finished; sides and false roof, $\frac{5}{16}$ in. finished; in red or white deal, pine or redwood. Back good 4 mm. plywood nailed outside.

DOOR: (a) size: 4 in. by 3½ in; (b) fasteners: one flat loop wire, 15 gauge, length 1½ in. outside, 1¼ in. inside, at bottom left-hand of door, ¾ in. from left edge and ¾ in. from bottom edge. One plain brass desk turn, 1 in. long fixed above top left-hand door in line with the loop wire fastener; (c) two strong brass hinges, 1 in. by ⅝ in. (when open) at right-hand side, fixed ¾ in. from top and bottom respectively; (d) to open ⅞ in. wire S-hook, 16 gauge, in centre of door; (e) left-hand edge, top and bottom of door, sloping bevel cut; right-hand edge straight cut (to take hinges); 3¾ in. overall from cage bottom, and centred with sides.

FRONT RAIL: (a) height 2¾ in. from cage floor, (b) thickness of wood $\frac{5}{16}$ in. finished; (c) pot fixed on removable door, 3⅜ in. by ¾ in. sloping bevel cut; (d) door pull, ⅝ in. wire S-hook, 16 gauge.

DRINKER: White plastic, 2½ in. by 1½ in. with ¼ in. flange at each end and ⅝ in. deep.

PERCHES: (a) length 4½ in. overall, diameter $\frac{9}{16}$ in. finished; ends flush cut, not pointed or cone-shaped; (b) plain boss at back projecting ½ in. diameter, 1¼ in. not painted; (c) position: screw holes at back of cage to be 5½ in. from bottom, overall, and 4⅜ in. apart; perches at front then centre with the crossbar.

WIRE FRONT: (a) comprises 21 wires, 14 gauge, mesh ⅝ in. centre to centre (b) height of crossbar, 5½ in. overall, i.e. including bottom of cage; (c) for strength, double-punched, set ⅜ in. apart; (d) curve at top, ¾ in. bow; (e) fixing, three wires left as spikes at top and bottom.

TOP: (a) width approximately 5½ in. sufficiently wide to cover strengthening bar; (b) hand-hole, kidney-shaped, 3¼ in. by 1¼ in.; (c) height of sloping false roof, 8½ in. from floor of cage.

COLOUR: Inside and wire front, white; outside, black.

NAME: No maker's name or mark must appear on the cage.
Note As from May 1971 judges are instructed to disqualify birds shown in WELDED FRONT cages.

Show Preparation

After a successful breeding season all of us look forward, having trained the current year's stock, to entering the shows. Those who can present the best they have bred to full advantage will beat the remainder who have neglected to work on their birds, which although of equal quality may be shown in dirty cages, may never have been trimmed or sprayed and may have feathering absent.

Cages

The show cage, even more than the aviary, is your shop window. There is nothing finer than to see an average bird beautifully staged and presented for judging, and while the cage itself is not judged, it does have an influence on the judge and the public. Every show season therefore should be preceded by full attention to every cage, no matter whether you have six or sixty. Each cage must be inspected for fading, since white paints do not remain brilliant white indefinitely; should they have faded, they should be resprayed or repainted immediately. Similarly any chipped or chewed areas must be refurbished and show fronts that have been badly chewed must be replaced.

The question of making any profit from exhibiting does not arise since any monetary gain can hardly compensate for the hours of work preceding it. It is more likely that you will incur a financial loss over the season, so prepare yourself for inevitable expenses but approach showing seriously enough to avoid being out of pocket every time.

At the beginning of each show season decide beforehand exactly which events you propose to enter. It is best to confine your attention to six events at the most, concentrating on the major open shows plus perhaps one or two others near at hand. Beginners or novices tend to show at local shows almost every weekend, especially if they are winning, sometimes to the extent that the birds tire rapidly and in the long run breed unsatisfactorily. It is important to remember that your birds eat the barest minimum at a show and are not at their best following even a one day event let alone three days at the National Show.

Removing broken or falling feathers

Knowing exactly the dates of the shows you wish to enter, you are in a position to select the complete team for the season, so work through the whole stud in June and remove all the tail feathers of the show team as chosen. You do not wish to have odd birds dropping one tail feather throughout the forthcoming months when by your action the risk can be avoided. Tail feathers take eight weeks to regrow, so by August, when the first major show is held, every bird has two perfect tail feathers. At intervals, also watch the spots and flights, removing them where necessary. If a spot has dropped on a favoured specimen you can be fairly sure the others will do so soon after. Anticipate this and remove the remaining spots, knowing that four weeks' growth will see a perfect necklace. Flights that are broken or frayed should be removed in the same way, allowing six to eight weeks for replacement.

Spraying

As the team is systematically worked over, put them into flight sections that were previously occupied as training areas for the current year stock. Needless to say these flights have to be thoroughly cleaned out first and every perch removed and scrubbed before replacement. When catching your birds you will notice that in the majority of cases they are thin and wiry and, certainly in the case of the youngsters, anything but steady. Put cocks and hens into separate flights and for the first week leave them alone to establish themselves and begin feeding on the good quality diet plus supplements normally given to the breeding team. After this settling-in period, transfer the group to one end of the flight cage, push in a slide and then soak the whole team thoroughly, using a pressure sprayer containing boiling water with added glycerin at the rate of one teaspoonful to each pint of water. This solution emerges as a warm and penetrating dense mist and after a thorough soaking the birds look a sorry sight. This complete, they are moved back to the dry section and allowed to dry naturally. In smaller studs it may be easier to use either a show cage or an old Yorkshire canary show cage for spraying purposes. The Yorkshire cages have the added advantage that you can spray each bird from all angles. Make sure your heavy spraying is carried out in the morning, giving the team ample time to dry during the day before roosting at night. Two or three days after this initial soaking, carry out the process again paying particular attention to the vent area, which is the area where loose feathering is most noticeable. By this time you should be about two weeks from the first show and during the next ten days you should spray three times a week, gradually lessening the amount as you do so. You will observe that the water now tends to run off the birds, because they have preened themselves in the process of drying, obtaining oil from a gland at the root of the tail. This oiling, aided by the glycerin in the sprayer, puts on the show sheen. Spraying should be withheld three days before the show and on the day prior to that last light spray, the final touches are made.

Hand washing

For some fanciers spraying is inadequate. Stock may be grubby from the use of cod liver oil soaked seed, or in industrial areas it may have become ingrained with deposited dirt. These people, and breeders of lutinos and albinos, are forced to resort to hand washing. If you are in doubt as to whether hand washing is necessary run the bird into a show cage; the white background will soon establish a decision one way or the other.

When you first tackle this job the only hazard, short of drowning the bird, is getting soap into its eyes. People do not care for this either, but budgies will automatically start scratching the eye area when they are returned to the drying cage and the result will be damaged, perhaps bloody eyelids.

Before beginning have ready three 8-in. diameter bowls containing lukewarm water, preferably water that has been boiled and is, as a result, softer. You also require a shaving brush and an old toothbrush; your receiving cages must be thoroughly clean as always. Lutino breeders sometimes put sheets of blotting paper on their cage floors to be absolutely sure of avoiding stains on the flights and tail feathers.

If you cover the floors with a thick layer of sawdust, this achieves the same object. Into the first bowl put a quantity of high grade shampoo and in the remaining bowls just lukewarm water. Do not have cooler water in the last bowl since, as you are totally immersing each bird, the effect of a sudden change of temperature is undesirable.

Holding the bird in the correct manner you are now ready to proceed. Slowly lower your hand into the water, keeping the head of the bird raised, and allow the bird to soak for about a minute. Next work over the breast and back with the shaving brush soaked in shampoo, moving with the grain of the feathers. This done, turn your attention to the flights; these should be spread down the side of the bowl and similarly stroked until you are satisfied. Pay attention to both sides of the flights and deal with the tail in the same way. Should any faeces have soiled the tail area then use the toothbrush first to clean this up quickly. Last of all wash the head, neck and mask, which is often the dirtiest area anyway and always the most difficult to deal with. The technique is identical, patience and care to avoid lather getting in the eyes being the main object. Try to keep your thumb well under the bird's beak to prevent it from chewing the brush when you are washing the mask. Once you are satisfied, drain off the surplus lather and immerse the bird into bowl number two and by spreading out the wings under the water and stroking the head area with the brush yet again most of the lather will be dispelled. A final rinse in the last bowl and the process is nearly finished. At this stage techniques differ, some fanciers preferring to use absorbent tissues and heat in the form of an infra-red heater directed on to the cage. I use neither, preferring the feathers to dry naturally and more slowly. If however you are forced by circumstances to hand wash in an evening then heat in some form must be used for they should not be left wet overnight. Never try to avoid washing the mask and head of the bird because it is the most difficult, otherwise the contrasting clean and dirty areas will be noticeable in the show cage.

Final preparations

If possible on the Wednesday preceding a weekend event, work through every member of the show team and remove the surplus spots which spoil the appearance of many birds. Under the Budgerigar Society rules you are permitted to 'remove' spots though any form of trimming is a breach of the rules. In other words the use of tweezers is permitted, while any indication of a scissor line on the mask or elsewhere has to be penalized by the judge. Spot removal is always approached by the beginner with trepidation since the inexperienced fancier can often remove one of the major spots accidentally, rendering the bird almost certainly without a chance of winning any specials for at least three to four weeks. Practise on non-important specimens from time to time when catching up birds for inspection in the birdroom.

Choose your tweezers carefully, the pointed serrated type are useless for this task, so buy a medium-sized pair of blunt-nosed, flat-faced tweezers and keep these on a length of string attached to the birdroom wall, where they can always be found. Assuming that you are right handed, hold the bird in your left hand with its back in your palm; close your hand round it gently and place your thumb under the 'jawline' to prevent the bird from biting you unnecessarily. Gloves should never be worn when handling a bird since you are unable to gauge your strength when wearing them, sometimes with fatal results. With the bird positioned you can remove the unwanted spots. Keeping the tweezers closed, slide them around the desired spot, opening them at the last second to allow the feather to slip between the flat surfaces. Try to grip the spot high up on the central vein and having grasped it move the tweezers slightly to ensure you have only the spot concerned and not the big important eye catcher next to it. If you are satisfied, give a firm pull and the process is complete. Often the inexperienced fancier will pull too early because he is unable to handle the bird correctly with his left hand and is being painfully bitten; in his haste to get the job done, out comes the wrong spot. Spot removal is a classic example of practice giving perfect results and eventually you should be able to do sixty birds in as many minutes.

The masks should now be perfect so turn your attention to the tails and flights. Are there any cracked major shafts? If so, and if they are not broken right through, but show just a bend mark, immerse the feather in boiling water for a second or two and it will straighten perfectly. Once every bird has had its final grooming give the team just a touch with the sprayer, cold water will be satisfactory, and you are ready for the weekend.

When caging up your team ready for transport pay attention to the birds as they go into the show cages. If you close the door on the tail of a bird the feathers will promptly come out, so be warned. Label your cages against the catalogue, checking that you have not labelled a grey green adult entry with, say, a grey green breeder's label as you do so, and then double check before you pack them for transport.

At the show itself, in the afternoon following judging, even if they have not done well that particular day give millet sprays to each cage. Budgerigars rarely eat correctly at shows and consequently lose weight to an enormous degree, particularly if it is a two-day show. They will always eat a millet spray with relish and it is well worth the trouble.

On returning home, even though you may be tired, complete your job properly; book in your results and return the team to their freshly cleaned flight cages, making sure they are amply supplied with fresh seed, water and grit, plus added cuttle. Nearly always when birds come back from shows they look for grit before anything else, so do not neglect to provide a fresh supply.

Exhibiting and the Exhibitor

Open shows/Members' shows
In the United Kingdom the budgerigar exhibitions are divided into two classifications, namely Members' Shows and Open Shows. Members' Shows are exhibitions at which members of that Society only can

exhibit their birds and generally one can find such Societies in most towns throughout the country. Normally Members' Shows have two important events, the Young Stock Show or Nest Feather Show sometime in June–July, followed by their Annual Show later in the year. It is usual for the members of one Society to belong to others in the surrounding districts with the object of trying to win at a series of shows in the summer or late autumn. At open Shows one does not need to be a member of the promoting Society to enter a team of birds. Open Shows attract higher quality birds than Members' Shows and they also have far bigger classes on the whole. At an Open Show you are effectively showing against the rest of the country, so to win Best Budgerigar in Show is quite an achievement. The Budgerigar Society Club Show is however an Open Show in a class by itself; it has in the region of four thousand exhibits, and attracts the highest quality budgerigars in the world. The other massive show held each year in London is the National Exhibition of Cage Birds and, while this encompasses other sections such as Canaries, British Birds and Foreign Exhibits, it has always been a highlight of the year, when some of the very best budgerigars are benched.

Status
Each exhibitor has to be graded according to the quality of his stock and his status may be that of Beginner, Novice, Intermediate or Champion. All four status are apparent at Open Shows but the Inter-mediate status is not always in use at Members' Shows. A newcomer obviously starts in the Beginner Classes in both Open and Members' Shows; subsequently many will find that their status is divided because progress has been made at the Members' events sufficient to move up to Novice, but this progress is still not enough to give the same status at an Open Show, so they remain Beginner Open Exhibitors. Each exhibitor has divided status for some years, the Members' Club Champion being an Intermediate at the bigger shows until he finally finishes up as an Open Champion Exhibitor.

Classes
All societies produce a schedule and entry form for their exhibitions and these are easily obtainable from their secretaries. Read the entry form thoroughly, since mistakes at the time of filling in the entry form are irritating later. You will find individuals and groups of colours classified under separate class numbers and they may or may not be separated into sexes. They normally range from the Light, Dark or

25 *A nest of fertile eggs, including some foster eggs from other pairs.*

26 *Well fed chicks at one and three days old respectively.*

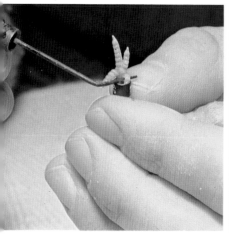

27 *Ringing with the aid of a rounded needle.*

28 *Lutino chicks with excellent downy growth (at about 18 days)*

29 *The author's aviary at Virginia Water.*

30 *Inside the author's aviary.*

31 *Outside flights in a Hampshire aviary.*

Olive Green group through all the colours until you arrive at the Any Other Variety section, into which goes any bird that is not covered elsewhere. The complete range of descriptions is normally set out twice, one for current year or breeders' classes and the other for adult birds of more than one year old. You may not enter purchased birds in breeders' classes even if they are current year birds and all birds shown in breeders' classes must have closed coded rings of the correct year as provided through the Budgerigar and Area Societies.

Completing entry forms
Absorb the schedule, take full note of the sexes and colours of the birds you wish to enter, then write in the column provided for descriptions of the exhibits the necessary information, checking the class number entered is correct depending on (a) your status (b) if a breeder exhibit or adult is being entered and (c) the sex of the exhibit. In the column headed 'Nominations' you may nominate birds you wish to enter for a particular trophy applicable to your status. The trophies available will be described in the schedule and depending on your birds' placing in their classes, you are awarded points, the exhibitor receiving the highest number winning the trophy concerned. The only remaining column on the form which may concern you is that asking you to price the exhibit. If you do so, the bird can be claimed by anyone, 10 per cent of the proceeds going to the Society. Should you not wish to sell them put 'N.F.S.' (not for sale) alongside each bird. Lastly, enter on the form any area societies of which you are a fully paid up member, stating your code number alongside, and of course his applies to Budgerigar Society membership as well. Finally check the whole form again, sign it and forward it to the secretary with the appropriate remittance; in a few days you will receive class labels, which should be fixed to each cage.

Transport
There are two methods of carrying your team to show by car. Either they may be placed in travelling boxes or the show cages may be packed loose in the car. Should you decide on the latter, ensure the floor is cushioned in some way for the first layer of cages. This will lessen any vibration and give 'first timers' a better chance of winning. Having filled the car, cover the whole group with a car blanket or black sheet to prevent the inevitable flashing lights of other vehicles disturbing your stock.

Railing birds is a different matter and obviously all cages have to be
6

boxed. Travelling boxes designed to carry three show cages to each box are the most practical. They are easily handled and not too heavy when full and are the most economical size to transport by rail. The railways are usually most helpful, especially if you are considerate enough to take your consignment to the station at an off-peak period. The boxes should have snap locks and straps securing them and nothing further. Any form of padlocking is impracticable; the stewards at shows cannot be expected to start hunting for keys when they have perhaps several hundred boxes to unpack. Each case should be labelled with the travelling card provided by the promoting society. These are filled in with the appropriate cage numbers and are checked by the stewards and signed on arrival.

When you first send your birds by rail you may be very concerned for their safety, especially as the consignment probably contains the cream of your stock. However the only worry is that they may become delayed en route and not arrive in time for judging. I have not heard of losses on the railway for many years and local station staff are often interested to find out how well you have done after a show.

When finally packing your team into the travelling boxes, ensure your labels are placed centrally on the front rail and are well stuck on, (do not rely on the gum on labels or they may have fallen off when the cages reach the show). Make sure the cages fit well into the boxes and that each rests on foam padding to cushion any shocks. Foam pads, or newspaper balls, can be wedged round the cages as well and the stewards when repacking for the return journey will use these wedges in the same way. Remember – secure packing helps you to win.

12. Judging

Ever since budgerigars were first put on public exhibition it has been apparent that the placing of them in order of merit has been one of the most criticized and debated tasks that falls to any fancier.

The Budgerigar Society has a written and pictorial 'Ideal Budgerigar', and these are regularly brought to the attention of every fancier through the media. Until subjected to further alteration the Ideal must, of necessity, remain the standard of excellence when placing awards at all shows whether large or small. There is always a body of opinion in the fancy that will say that the present Ideal has been superseded by specimens which take best in show awards. When this opinion is held by the majority of the fancy, then and only then can a change be sought through the Budgerigar Society Council. On the last occasion, five leading judges were appointed to produce the new Ideal, and they produced an excellent profile. In pictorial form a frontal or three-quarter view would be useful to newcomers to the hobby and this may be considered in the future. These would help to give all exhibitors the correct impression of width in the champion sense.

Exhibitors must realize that the judges can only place in order what is put in front of them. Specimens that are superior to others in the class have to be given awards even if not perfect examples of the current 'Ideal'. Because certain top breeders continually turn out birds that are better than anyone else's, there is a tendency for these breeders to sway the fancy away from the Ideal with certain show features. There is, however, no doubt that very few, if any, budgerigars have ever been exhibited which in all points equal the Ideal. Judges are required to interpret the Ideal Budgerigar against each individual specimen with which they are confronted to the best of their ability, depending on what good and bad show points the bird is showing *at that moment*.

Exhibitors should also appreciate, on this question of interpretation, that no two people see details alike even if both are looking at a bird at the same time. Add to this the time lag from when the judge sees the bird in the morning to when the owner sees it in the afternoon, after it has been settled for an hour or so, and it becomes obvious why judges are criticized. The chances are that if a judge were asked to re-assess a placing in the afternoon, he would probably agree that a particular bird could have gone up a place or two. A sobering thought is that a judge will never be asked to reconsider a bird placed *too* highly.

Not all judges are beyond criticism. There has always been a body of opinion that to be a good judge you must also be a breeder and exhibitor while you act in this capacity. Many judges have bred budgerigars perhaps twenty or thirty years previously and some of these have moved with the times and are still efficient; others unfortunately still persist, because they no longer exhibit themselves, in judging to old standards, to the disenchantment of the current exhibitors. In the light of this the Budgerigar Society rules have been amended with effect from 1974 to read as follows:

1. That a judge must be a member of the Budgerigar Society for ten years.
2. That there should be a once only registration fee to be agreed upon.
3. That all judges should be current breeders and exhibitors of Budgerigars and that they should have reached champion status.
4. That entry should be through a subsidiary panel and for the first three years a judge can only judge special, rosette and approved patronage shows.
5. That they must apply for admission to the main panel after the third year giving details of shows judged and applicants should be vetted by the Judges Panel Committee.
6. That those who have not adjudicated at a B.S. patronage show for a minimum of three years are automatically omitted from the Judges Panel.

From the judges' point of view

It is of course impossible to please every exhibitor, since somebody has to be second or out of the cards. The only satisfied exhibitor is the one who is first or goes on to take special prizes; as a result a judge has to be fairly thick skinned and be able to satisfactorily explain to critics the reasons for poor placings.

All judges should be capable of judging every variety and must make themselves fully conversant with the lesser known colours, even though they themselves do not breed these varieties. Good coloured yellows, for instance, are often of mediocre quality while those appearing the best headed and superior in type are likely to be suffused with a greenish tinge. Although points are not awarded directly, as in the Continental system of judging, a judge should be aware in the back of his mind of the 'Scale of Points' as published in this country and apply it consciously to all varieties.

Some judges have long memories and are heard quoting an exhibit's past achievements. This is wrong since every bird has its day and the following week will have dipped. Assuming there is a better bird than last week's champion, the judge who does not have the courage to act as he should for fear of what others might say will never be respected. As a breeder and exhibitor, a judge should be aware exactly which points are the most difficult to establish and full credit must go to the man who has had the skill to put those salient features together in one bird. This may have taken him years and years of breeding and all credit goes to the winner of the 'Best Breeder' special at any show.

When a judge enters a show he may have just travelled for two or three hours, having risen very early, and the thought of five hours concentration on moving birds is sometimes appalling. However, once started with an efficient group of stewards behind him, that time passes in a flash. He must be in full command of his stewards, not permitting any 'loose advice' to come from them. There is no need to be tight lipped; he may sometimes explain verbally his reasons for positioning a bird, but always anything stated should be of a constructive nature designed to help and teach those watching.

The easiest classes to judge are usually those in the Champion Section where faults have been reduced to a large degree. The further down the grades one progresses the more difficult it becomes until once in the beginner section the judge is balancing against each other large numbers of faults in every bird. Yet attention and time must be given fairly to all sections since the beginner has paid the same as the champion for the privilege of exhibiting.

Finally the judge has to be a slick administrator to deal efficiently with all the paper work which accompanies a show. If he appears confused to the officials this will not stand him in good stead so he must endeavour to learn this aspect thoroughly before starting. He must also be decisive and get through quickly so that he does not hold up fellow judges. There is nothing more infuriating than to have to wait for a judge who takes two hours longer than necessary, which results in later classes being judged after the public have been admitted.

Judging a class

Assume, as an example, you are the judge and are judging your first breeders' class of the morning. You are confronted with twenty light green normal cock birds from which you have to extract seven and place them in order. Before any judging takes place your first action should be to check there are no birds incorrectly classed either by

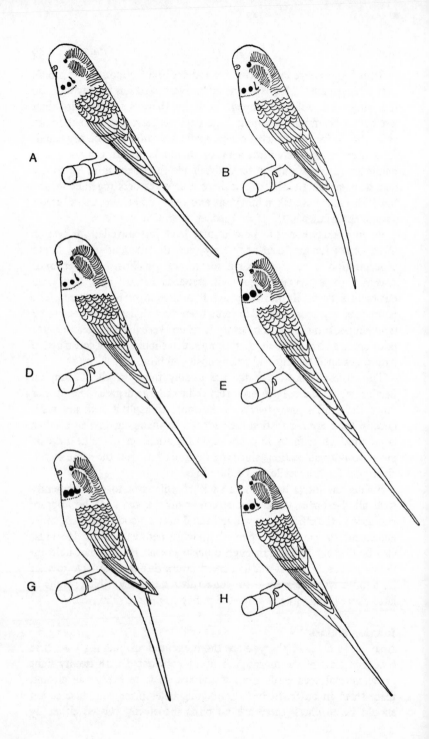

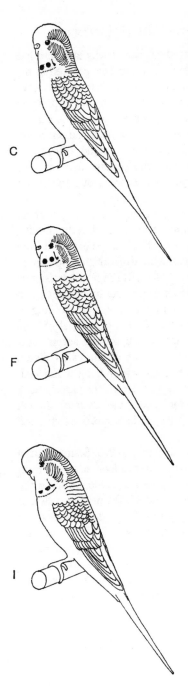

Some common budgerigar faults

A *A good back line but a poor angle on the perch; small spots.*

B *Hinged tail; small spots.*

C *Nipped-in neck.*

D *Excessive weight in the region of the chest spoiling the outline; small spots.*

E *A typical long-flighted bird with excessive tail length and extra primaries in the wings.*

F *Short mask.*

G *Spots overlarge and touching; crossed flights and hinged tail.*

H *A poor head.*

I *A large head with undesirable half-moon spots, but a good depth of mask.*

colour or sex. Second, since this is a breeders' class, check each bird has a closed coded ring of the correct colour. You can now proceed to the actual judging. First impressions are the best so your initial move should be to glance at every bird quickly and take a mental impression of what is before you. It may be there are six or seven which you can see automatically are way behind the rest, so extract those first and put them, in view, on another table set alongside the judging stand. Turn your attention then to the other end of the scale and perhaps there are five or six in this upper category. These you put in one group to the left of the stand. You are now left with a middle group, which for the moment ignore. Now examine the upper group in detail, again working from both superior and inferior ends until you are left with the middle, where a more difficult decision has to be made. Find the best bird from the original middle group and set it against the worst of the top group, rejecting it or inserting it into the correct place. If the latter decision is taken yet another comes from the middle group and so on, until you are satisfied. All new judges should adopt this policy of working at opposite ends of the quality scale, since it saves a great deal of time that would otherwise be wasted. A final check on the seven birds placed, and a confirmatory glance at those out of the cards before instructing the stewards to remove them, and the judging is finished. The results are marked on each cage and recorded in the judge's book and the first placed exhibit retained for special awards later. It will then reappear, perhaps before another judge, in its respective status and age group.

Always try to visualize, even subconsciously, the B.S. Standard, as a living model with width, and always remember to look at a bird from the front since the quality does not lie just in the profile. Some of the exhibits pictured in this book give examples of this feature but it should be remembered that even these are not perfect. Perfection is something we cannot reach with livestock, there is always room for improvement.

In conclusion do not eliminate birds for a spot missing or one tail feather missing. Penalize it by all means, according to what the point is worth on the Scale of Points, but remember it can regrow. A bird can always grow another feather, but it cannot grow another head.

13. Selling Surplus Stock

At the end of each year we all have a quantity of surplus stock which can be sold to bring revenue to buy foodstuffs and new outcrosses for the next season. As one would expect, the champions find it easier to dispose of their stock than do beginners, and beginners may seem unable to sell any birds at all. It usually materializes that they have not really got down to telling anyone they have birds for sale. An advertisement in the weekly magazine, *Cage and Aviary Birds*, will usually do the trick and there are quarterly bulletins produced by the Budgerigar Society and Area Societies where your name can easily appear.

Many people hesitate to advertise in case this involves them in despatching birds to customers 'on approval'. There is a degree of work entailed when you receive such a request but it is not that great. Assuming you decide to send stock by rail, you must be prepared in advance and obtain an adequate number of rail boxes. These are normally made of strong cardboard and average 8 in. by 5 in. by 5 in. You will also need livestock labels and a pad of despatch forms from your local station.

When a request for your birds arrives, reply stating exactly when the birds will be despatched, making certain the letter has time to arrive before you send the birds. On the agreed date, take the boxed livestock and despatch form to your station at an off-peak period and the bird will reach its destination within twenty-four hours. All labels should be clearly addressed; if possible arrange for the purchaser to collect the consignment at his end, marking the label 'to be called for'. It is normal for birds to be on approval for three days to the customer. This gives the stock a chance to settle on arrival (they will probably take a full day to recover their original quality after travelling by rail). Should the birds not be required they must be returned within the stipulated time otherwise the seller is entitled to retain the money originally sent to him against the value of the birds. If you make quite sure you have the money from the buyer *before* you despatch, and return it once a bird is sent back, all will be well. Trouble starts only when the buyer is *not* asked to forward a deposit. One last word on the railing of stock – do send birds in new boxes as this will create a good impression and an indication of how the stock is kept.

When writing to customers try to include a brief description of the good and bad points of each bird, so that the buyer has some idea of what to expect; but be factual and do not exaggerate, otherwise when the bird does arrive it will be promptly returned. Show results are always helpful if available, and try also to give a choice of birds and a price range as well as this is always well received.

Pricing your stock can sometimes be difficult at first, but as you become experienced you will see the points which go towards giving any budgerigar the value set upon it. Some fanciers price on blood lines, others on the visual qualities of the birds.

14. Diseases

All fanciers will eventually be faced with a bird which has succumbed to some form of disease. Most veterinarians will give first-class treatment and advice to owners of both large and small studs, so do not hesitate to contact your nearest surgery should there be the slightest possibility that a bird might be lost.

In order to recognize sickness and understand some of the symptoms, one book which all bird fanciers should buy is Stroud's *Digest on the Diseases of Birds*. This was written by Robert Stroud in America and first published in 1943. It was the culmination of many years' work studying all forms of disease which affect birds and today it is still accepted as the greatest contribution on this subject. Robert Stroud wrote it while a convict in the prison of Alcatraz in San Francisco, and considering the conditions under which this volume was written, one can only pay tribute to a great bird fancier. (Stroud has been immortalized in the film *The Birdman of Alcatraz*.) The book is out of date in that modern drug treatment has superseded the methods advocated by Stroud, but on the subject of diagnosis it is still to be thoroughly recommended.

Every birdroom should possess one of two methods which can be employed to assist a sick bird to overcome any contracted disease. This should be either a hospital cage or an infra-red lamp, both providing heat to the chilled bird. Warmth is of great benefit to any ill budgerigar and is an important aid to recovery. The type of hospital cage sold today consists of upper and lower compartments separated by a grill. The lower contains one or two light bulbs providing the heat, which rises and maintains a good heat in the upper berth where the sick bird is situated.

If using a hospital cage, do ensure that adequate ventilation is available in addition to the warmth applied. Many birds have been lost simply because the sick bird has become dehydrated. Fanciers expect that because of the heat the bird will become thirsty and drink adequately; what happens, however, is the reverse – because the bird is ill it does not always obey its normal instincts and therefore dehydrates. A common occurrence with birds which suffer from severe enteritis is that the curing drug, plus the dehydration, result in the bird surviving but going blind.

To avoid this danger of dehydration it is perhaps preferable to use an infra-red heater fastened to the front of an ordinary cage. This allows the bird to choose a position most suited to its needs and there is room for it to move out of the area of direct heat if it wishes.

Causes and symptoms of disease

Diseases of birds can be attributed to six major causes.

1 Viruses
2 Bacteria
3 Moulds
4 Nutrition
5 Parasites
6 Poisons

Whatever the cause, sick birds initially always display the same symptoms and success with treatment is naturally more likely the sooner the sick bird is spotted. Make a routine of looking at every bird in the aviary once a day. Once you are familiar with the early symptoms described below it becomes an easy matter, even when glancing over several hundred budgerigars, to pick out the unwell specimen. If any of your stock display any of the following symptoms, the bird should be caught and examined further.

1 Huddled appearance
2 Feathers raised, particularly those on the back
3 Head appears to be drawn down into the body and the spot line stands out instead of lying flat
4 A 'pumping' tail action, indicating respiratory difficulties
5 Soiled vent

Diagnosis

Having caught the bird you suspect is sick you now have to decide exactly the cause of the problem and whether you are capable of treating the bird successfully. The colour and consistency of the droppings should be examined. The mouth should be looked at for signs of wetness other than from recent drinking and the breathing should be considered. Lastly check whether the bird has a full crop and whether the breastbone is rounded or sharp. An ailing bird confirmed, it should be isolated in another birdroom. This way a possible epidemic can be avoided and you are in a strong position to prevent cross-infection to the main flock. After handling a sick bird, clean the flight or cage and thoroughly wash your hands.

E. Coli infection

Escherichia Coli is a bacterium which invades the gut of young chicks and may be present in high numbers, not necessarily causing any harm. A chick when born does not have any living organisms in the gut but within a few days the gut will become colonized. Trouble only arises when these bacteria, instead of remaining in the gut, invade the body via the bloodstream and produce an infection. Not all the answers are known regarding the habits of this bacterium and the scientists are as yet unable to make definite suggestions to prevent deaths.

Symptoms

The bird will have all the usual budgerigar appearances of being unwell, with a reluctance to move and closed eyes. Yellowish diarrhoea may be present. There is sometimes difficulty in breathing but there is no discharge from the nostrils.

Post mortem examination

The skin will have a dry, shrunken look and appear to stick to the underlying flesh instead of moving over it. The heart pericardium (i.e. the surrounding membrane) will be thickened and opaque and the heart will have a deposit of fibrous material. The liver and kidneys will be swollen, the liver sometimes being coated with a gelatinous fluid. Unfortunately many of these symptoms are also those present in other diseases so a laboratory diagnosis must be obtained.

Treatment

Laboratory advice must be sought since many types of E. Coli are resistant to common antibiotics. The laboratory should be able, once the bacterium has been isolated, to recommend the most suitable drug.

Salmonella infection

Salmonella is a group of bacteria comprising several hundred types, including human typhoid. It can give rise to serious epidemics amongst birds both in the wild and in captivity. It is important to remember that the salmonella bacteria from birds will have little significance to man unless eaten. Half-cooked chicken is a well-known cause of salmonella food poisoning as one in seven chickens is known to suffer from this at some stage during its life.

Symptoms

The disease is mainly restricted to young birds. They display a dejected appearance, are listless and weak. They huddle together with lowered heads and the vents may be plastered with white excreta. Some die quickly, others are stunted before recovering.

Post mortem examination

The liver will be found to be enlarged and mottled.

Sources of infection and treatment

Birds that recover from salmonella infection may be carriers since the bacteria can last up to a year in their internal organs. Their droppings if ingested are the source of danger to other birds, since the bacteria can survive for many weeks outside the body. If infected birds are used for breeding the salmonella can infect the eggs by penetration of the shell, so it must be realized that this disease can move very swiftly through any stud. A laboratory test will quickly establish the salmonella infection. A new drug, Furazolidone, has proved ideal to combat this infection but veterinary advice should be sought before dosage.

Avian tuberculosis

This is not a frequent infection in caged birds but under such restricted conditions as an aviary the disease is chronic and develops slowly. Permanent loss of condition is the first sign; raised feathers and persistent diarrhoea may be common. Some birds refuse to move about, others waste and eventually after a prolonged illness may die.

Post mortem examination

There will be severe wasting of the muscular tissues of the body and the liver and spleen will be covered with greyish white nodules which may extend to the intestine.

Sources

Avian tuberculosis can be contracted from droppings of wild birds which fall into the outside flights or from an introduced bird suffering from the early stages of the disease.

Diagnosis

This has to be effected by a laboratory test which is quite simple. Once confirmed, vigorous culling should be employed and all carcasses burnt. The aviary must then be scrubbed out with hot water containing 10 per cent formalin solution before any stock is reintroduced.

Aspergillosis

This occurs both in wild and caged birds and is a fungal disease of the lungs. It is likely to arise where the stock is kept under insanitary conditions. The favoured deep litter method of breeding can bring about this disease. The fungus concerned is called Aspergillus fumigatus and resembles those fungi seen on bread. It is inhalation of the spores that causes the disease, the spores growing in the lungs in almost the same way as they do under outside damp conditions.

Symptoms

The birds are weak and stand about with feathers ruffled. They have a poor appetite and great thirst. As the disease progresses emaciation occurs and they have difficulty in breathing, to the extent of gasping, wheezing and fighting for breath. The death rate can be as high as 90 per cent of the stud.

Post mortem examination

The lungs and air passages will have masses of greyish-white nodules throughout.

Treatment

This is a question largely of prevention rather than cure, since affected birds do not respond to antibiotics or other related drugs. Hygienic conditions must prevail and any affected birds be destroyed if the disease is to be overcome.

Psittacosis

This is a virus disease affecting parrotlike species but due to the strict importation controls in the U.K. the disease rarely manifests itself in aviaries in this country. The controls are necessary since psittacosis can be contracted by man by inhalation, though proven cases of psittacosis are rare nowadays. The symptoms are easily confused in budgerigars with an upper respiratory infection and can only be diagnosed accurately by a laboratory. Any inference from an outside source that a fancier's aviary is infected should be substantiated by isolation of the virus under laboratory control before permission to destroy the stud is given.

Diseases of the respiratory tract

The lungs and other organs of respiration are susceptible to infections which can spread quite quickly throughout a stud unless strict control is observed. These diseases may be anything from a cold to bronchitis or even pneumonia, or may arise from fungal sources such as aspergillosis. The nares (nostrils) frequently become blocked, and this is usually accompanied by discharge from the eyes, sneezing and a droopy, chilled appearance with a reluctance to feed. If observed early and the bird is given heat this may be adequate to restore the bird to fitness. If worse and the bird obviously has difficulty in breathing, which he shows by gasping and a pumping action of the tail, then administration of an antibiotic such as Terramycin or Chloromycetin Palmitate at the rate of one drop to the mouth twice daily will usually bring about spectacular results. Veterinary confirmation should be sought.

Coccidiosis

Coccidiosis is probably the most prevalent infectious disease in budgerigars and can result in a large number of deaths. It is caused by living organisms called coccidia and there are many types in existence. Those affecting budgerigars cannot infect other varieties of birds and the reverse is also true. There are two main types of infection, caecal and intestinal, depending on the part of the gut affected.

Coccidia have a life cycle within the birds and outside. The cycle where the coccidia are transferred from bird to bird is called the oocyst stage. These oocysts are passed out in the droppings of an infected bird and are ingested by birds which eat those droppings. The oocysts are extremely resistant and may remain alive in the aviary for as long as eighteen months. They are not killed by ordinary disinfectants.

After the oocysts have been swallowed they develop, liberating new forms which invade the cells lining the gut. If the infestation is heavy, bleeding may arise. After rapid multiplication the secondary phase of sexual reproduction begins, in which sexual unions form the coccidial oocysts. These are then passed out of the bird and complete the cycle. Many studs are only lightly affected, with no noticeable signs of ill health, but once large numbers of oocysts are swallowed, particularly if the conditions of warmth and moisture which suit the coccidia persist, then adverse signs will be apparent.

If the stock is maintained under good standards of hygiene with plenty of room and fresh air then all should be well. Frequent removal of the droppings must be the general practice. If this is carried out the stud will gradually build up its own immunity, those most likely to be affected being young birds.

Intestinal coccidiosis

This usually occurs in chicks from six weeks to six months old. Affected birds have diarrhoea but do not pass blood. The appetite is poor and they gradually waste and become emaciated. Their condition will be poor. Diagnosis should be by laboratory inspection and the best form of treatment will be allied to the identification of the kind of coccidia.

Treatment

Prevention by regular cleaning is the rule, so that infections remain light and result in immunity. The sulphonamide drugs are however good, the most popular being Sulphaquinoxaline. This is marketed under the brand name of 'Embazin' and is remarkably effective, providing stock is not overdosed.

Enteritis

This scourge of the budgerigar is the cause of more deaths than perhaps any other disease. Many birds are found every year with a huddled appearance and green stained vent area, which if not observed within a short space of time results in the quick death of the bird. The onset of enteritis is often caused by a chill, an infective agent or a dietary disturbance. Frequently the first signs of an illness that eventually becomes enteritis is a froth emerging from the mouth accompanied by a continuous spitting action. Once this early facial wetness is seen the bird should be isolated and one drop of Terramycin syrup (strength 125 mg. in 25 ml.) administered per day. If caught early the bird should recover within twenty-four hours, but a full course of five days' treatment should be given to prevent a recurrence. If however the bird has been overlooked and is seriously ill, the dosage can be put up to 3 drops per day. The hospital cage must be used carefully, ensuring the bird does not become dehydrated. Warm water with added glucose given by dropper direct to the beak will be of considerable help from time to time, maintaining strength and avoiding dehydration while the drug takes effect. Should the bird recover but be blind as sometimes occurs, it is because the bird has suffered from dehydration during the illness.

Tumours

Very common, particularly with older pet birds, these growths may be either benign tumours or malignant cancerous growths. They are usually found in the vent area, though they may occur elsewhere. The most common, though not seen, is a tumour found at the base of the brain on the pituitary gland; this is normally benign. Veterinary surgeons can operate successfully on benign tumours provided they are not permitted to become excessively large. Malignant tumours are inoperable.

Fractures

The wing

A fracture in the wing of a budgerigar is less common than one in the leg, but when it does occur it is normally in the junction of the middle and lower thirds of the humerus. Veterinary attention is advisable since the use of an anaesthetic may be necessary to avoid extensive shock while the wing is splinted. Many fanciers simply isolate the bird and leave it to its own resources, allowing the damage to repair of its own accord. Invariably however there is a dropping or high-slung wing appearance after such a break.

The leg

A break in the humerus is usually allowed to heal itself. If the fracture is compound, amputation by a qualified surgeon is necessary. Lower leg fractures can usually be dealt with without veterinary help, using a feather quill as a splint placed longitudinally down to the leg around a cotton wool press. Disinfect and dress the leg carefully beforehand and take care the splint is not too tight, else gangrene will quickly set in.

Going light

This term is used frequently by fanciers to describe the wasting appearance of a sick bird suffering from severe loss of body weight and a ravenous appetite. It does not refer to a single disease, but to one of fourteen possible diseases all of which give rise to the same symptoms. These diseases are:

1 Air sac mites
2 Aspergillosis
3 Cancer in pigeons
4 Kidney disease
5 Parasites – external
6 Parasites – internal
7 Paratyphoid
8 Poisoning (e.g. from excess vitamins)
9 Pseudotuberculosis
10 Pullorum disease
11 Toxoplasmosis
12 Tuberculosis
13 Tumours
14 Starving

External parasites

Mites have a complicated life cycle. The adults, which are visible to the naked eye, lay eggs which hatch into an immature form. These young mites then live through a number of moults before maturing. They live on blood and tissue fluid extracted from their hosts and can transmit certain diseases from bird to bird by their feeding habits. The most notorious form is the red mite but there are others such as depluming mites, scaly leg mites and fodder mites.

The Red Mite

Perhaps the most common of mites, these live in daylight hours in the numerous cracks in cages and aviaries. Any crevice, be it the end of a perch, the joints of a nest box, the underside of the cage trays, can conceal red mite. When they have not eaten they are white to pale grey in colour but when they have consumed blood they are dark red. They are able to live for months without feeding and emerge at night, crawling along the perches and infesting the roosting birds. Having had their fill they return the same way as day approaches. This secretive habit can cause severe damage to the stud without the owner being aware. There are several aerosol sprays available containing Malathion or Pyrethrum preparations which if used carefully can quickly eradicate the infestation.

Depluming Mites

These creatures live at the base of feathers and produce intense irritation to the extent that an infected bird may pull out its own feathers or break them off at the base. Certain birds denude themselves in completely accessible areas. Depluming mites are not common. If the disease is suspected, dip the bird in warm soapy water containing sulphur daily for about a week, and spray the cage or aviary with anti-mite solution.

Scaly Mite

This mite gives rise, both on the legs and around the beak, to a condition known as 'scaly face'. It is a mange mite which burrows under the skin and causes thick growths, first seen as white patches, on the legs, at the corners of the mouth and under the lower mandible. If allowed to remain there the resulting build up of the crust-like formation can cause permanent damage. Once spotted the mite can quickly be killed by two or three applications of Benzyl Benzoate applied with a brush. Smothering the area with liquid paraffin may suffocate the mites in due course, but tends to cause intestinal trouble as the bird preens itself.

Mites – Conclusions

Apart from sprays and solutions sold for the purpose of ridding mites, regular painting and decorating of the aviary once a year will certainly help to control infestation. If all trays, nest boxes and perches are also scrubbed well with hot water and disinfectant before the breeding season the numbers will be drastically reduced. Mites cannot be starved out just because the breeding cages are empty, they have to be cleaned out. Budgerigars do not in general bathe, therefore control of the mites has to be carried out by the breeder if he wants his stock to live in comfort. Red mite have been accused of contributing to, if not being the sole cause of, French moult (see page 168.)

Internal parasites: worms

High quality egg contents and subsequent increased growth rate can never be achieved if the adults are harbouring internal parasites in the form of roundworms that inhabit the alimentary tract. Tapeworms are also found in parrotlike species but are not so common. Roundworms come into two basic categories, the large $1\frac{1}{2}$ in. roundworms found in budgerigars, termed Ascaridia, and hairlike roundworms called Capillaria. The former are easily found on post-mortem, but the latter are not easily distinguishable from the normal bowel contents. Capillaria live embedded by the hundred in the bowel wall, absorbing the nutrients that pass over them to the detriment of their host. The same applies to the Ascaridia, except of course that being a much larger species there are by no means as many within the gut, two or three worms being the normal amount.

The adult worms reproduce by laying thousands of eggs and these are passed out with the bird's droppings on to the aviary floor where they undergo a slow or quick 'ripening' process dependent on the air temperature. When ripe eggs are eaten by other birds they hatch within the bowel, causing severe inflammation, after which the young worms grow and reach maturity in six to eight weeks. By this time these worms also start laying eggs and it is easy to understand how an aviary can become infected throughout. Unfortunately these tiny worm eggs are easily transferred, either by the aviary attendant's feet or simply in the air, so that once an aviary is infected they are not easily eradicated. The first treatment is to use a 10 per cent solution of ammonia, scrubbing the flights and cage trays thoroughly, but take care that the birds are removed first and do not inhale an excessive amount of ammonia fumes yourself.

Birds that are infected have all the classic symptoms of 'going light', including general weakness and emaciation, severe loss of condition, lowered egg production when breeding and perhaps diarrhoea. Treatment of such birds can be by a 3 per cent solution of Nilverm which can be obtained from most chemists, administered direct to the beak. Dose with 0·5 ml. dilute Nilverm (1 part Nilverm to 6 parts water) every twenty-four hours for a maximum of three days, by which time the bird will have expelled any worms present. Piperazine Citrate is another suitable drug but veterinary advice should be taken before its use.

All outside flights should be covered with translucent sheeting to prevent infection from wild birds, which are known to carry worm infection. Some breeders today make a practice of de-worming annually but there is little point in this unless a flock has been infected on some previous occasion.

Nutritional diseases

Food deficiences, both partial and complete, can give rise in all mammals and birds to specific diseases. When feeding stock under artificial conditions it is common for not only deficiencies but also excesses of certain items to have adverse effects. As we have seen in the chapter on feeding, a diet that is satisfactory for the non-breeding bird can be totally inadequate under intensive breeding conditions, but even then it is important that the ingredients be present in adequate but not excessive amounts.

Experiments with proteins and vitamins may result in both good and bad effects. One effect of vitamins given in excess is that the absorption of other items, for example potassium or protein, is blocked. The appearance of birds suffering from this is in some cases symptomatic of an infectious disease and to track down the correct cause is often difficult. Nutritional diseases are more likely to be apparent in young chicks from birth to six months and certainly account for chicks aged between three and five weeks that are found dead in the nest box with no apparent cause.

VITAMIN A DEFICIENCY

Adults and more especially chicks are drowsy and lack vigour. Their growth rate is at first very slow and then ceases. Their general condition is poor, the ceres being almost white and the eyes tend to have a watery discharge which coagulates. The death rate can be high. Fish liver oils are an excellent source of Vitamin A if given in moderation. Deficiency of Vitamin A causes reduced hatchability.

VITAMIN A EXCESS

If too much Vitamin A is given it accumulates in the body and the majority is stored in the liver; if consumed in grossly excessive amounts it is acutely toxic. Lack of appetite, poor feather growth and swollen wings and leg joints may be apparent. Continuous administration of seed totally covered by fish oils can easily cause this condition.

VITAMIN B DEFICIENCY

The Vitamin B group covers a number of substances and it is not easy to differentiate the individual Vitamin B deficiencies from one another. As a generalization, the principal symptoms include retardation of growth and poor feathering, loss of appetite and upsetting of the nervous system. This latter symptom may be seen in the form of inability to retain balance, jerky movements and partial paralysis. Dried yeast and milk are excellent natural sources and coupled with the use of Abidec and Cytacon adequately cover the B group.

VITAMIN C DEFICIENCY

Many fanciers dispense with the use of the greenfoods which are the richest source of this vitamin. This has given rise in some studs to the equivalent of scurvy in people, which manifests itself by the joints becoming tender and swollen and breathlessness. The feet become noticeably thicker and scaly and the birds are generally weak. Studs such as this however are few and far between since the administration of Abidec (containing ascorbic acid) prevents its onset. Rose-hip syrup in moderation is also an excellent source of Vitamin C but take care in using this, as its action is scouring. There is no real substitute for greenfood from an uncontaminated source especially if available in the form of chickweed.

VITAMIN D DEFICIENCY

Absence of this vitamin gives rise to rickets. The legs become deformed and the birds are unable to fly. Vitamin D is easily supplied by fish oil, but it is also important to remember that rickets can arise as a result of unbalanced or inadequate supplies of calcium and phosphorus. Lack of sunlight, which reacts on the skin to form Vitamin D, can also cause this disease.

VITAMIN D EXCESS

Excessive use of fish oils results in chicks which lose their appetite, vomit and subsequently waste away. In extreme cases, where perhaps large quantities of wheat germ oil have been added to cod liver oil, death is a distinct possibility.

VITAMIN E DEFICIENCY

In the absence of Vitamin E budgerigar eggs do not hatch properly and the chicks that do survive may die of brain injury and an accumulation of fluid in their tissues. This is known as the anti-sterility vitamin and is sometimes added to the diet in the form of wheat germ oil, since this also has the ability to act as an anti-oxidant for such substances as Vitamin A. Its use in minimal quantities can be tried, but only when deficiency of this vitamin is proven. An excess of fish oil can destroy Vitamin E with resulting infertility.

Miscellaneous disorders

PROLAPSE

Prolapse of the vent can be caused by egg binding, inflammation of the oviduct or the strain of continual laying. The condition is made apparent by the appearance of tissue extending from the vent. Treatment is by washing the exposed part in dilute disinfectant and attempting to replace the parts by gentle pressure. The bird should on no account be used again for breeding for at least twelve months.

IODINE DEFICIENCY

In the early 1960s, as a result of some intensive work by Dr D. K. Blackmore, B.Sc., F.R.C.V.S., it was discovered that a high proportion of birds had enlarged or diseased thyroid glands (this fact had also been observed earlier by Dr Greyer of the Munich Veterinary School). Analysis showed that 85 per cent of pet birds were affected and 20 per cent died as a direct cause. This disease is called thyroid dysplasia. Against these figures it was later found that 21 per cent of breeders' birds were also affected. A normal gland is about five millimetres at its broadest point whereas a diseased gland can be up to four times that size; this increased growth can be caused by blood pressure, respiratory problems or digestive difficulties. Sometimes the gland ruptures and the bird bleeds to death internally.

Breeders who feed fish oil additives have no worries since there is a good iodine content contained in this but in ordinary seed diets the iodine content is inadequate. Iodized vitamin blocks are now available to assist those who do not feed any form of fish oil.

French moult

This disease, which is currently thought to be caused by poor nutrition, manifests itself in young birds from four to seven weeks old. It appears both towards the end of the period when the chicks are still in the nest box and shortly thereafter. It consists of the breakdown of the feather shafts at the point where they enter the flesh, which results in the shafts fracturing at those points. The principal feathers affected are the primaries, secondaries and tail feathers though in extreme cases the body feathers are also affected. The term French moult was derived from the fact that birds in Europe were known to suffer from this problem, and exported birds from France were at one time thought to carry the disease in a hidden form.

Since the affected birds are eventually unable to fly they are termed 'runners'. Depending on the severity of the problem birds may recover and grow new feathers but diagnosis is often too late, with the result that the tip of the broken feather remains in the follicle, preventing a new feather from emerging. For many years fanciers were under the impression that dipping such runners in warm disinfectant cured the problem, though what was actually occurring was the softening of the residual feather stumps which helped the new growth to emerge.

All birds should be examined in the nest at regular intervals from three weeks onwards, paying particular attention to the bases of the primaries. If any sign of a black dried blood core appearing in the shafts of the primaries is seen, the primaries, secondaries and tail feathers should be withdrawn immediately. In nearly every case the new growth will be perfect and quite normal, only where the stumps have been left in will there be any gaps in the normal wing feather complement. Dipping in mild disinfectant followed by thorough rinsing also helps; the birds are then cleared of mites and their bodies are able to put all their resources into the new feathering.

Why this phenomenon happens every few years in breeding establishments has caused hours of discussion and years of work by research scientists, not the least of whom is Dr T. G. Taylor, M.A., Ph.D., formerly of Reading University. While he has advanced the theory that the underlying cause is poor nutrition, this still remains unproven as he himself will admit. The school of thought opposed to the nutrition theory claims the red mite in some way contributes to the problem by withdrawing blood from the growing chick at the fundamental time when it is required for current feather growth. Let us examine the facts more closely.

1 A stud can remain unaffected by this complaint for years and then suddenly one season a percentage of French moulters appear.

2 One nest of birds may contain some affected birds while others remain quite normal.

3 Birds bred in the first round may be unaffected, yet some or even all of the second round will be French moulters.

4 If, for example, a nest of six eggs is divided equally and three eggs are transferred to a foster pair, those resulting chicks under the foster pair may be French moulters and those with the parents quite normal. Conversely those left with the parents may be French moulters and those reared by the fosters normal.

5 French moulters, when their feathers are examined, appear in some cases to be infected with microscopic mites not all of them red mites, yet unaffected birds reared in the same nest do not show this degree of infestation.

6 Both rounds can be affected with sometimes the second round being the most serious.

7 Birds suffering from French moult and subsequently 'cured' do not necessarily breed French moulters themselves.

8 The cleanliness or otherwise of a stud has no bearing whatsoever on the presence of French moult, the dirtiest and cleanest studs can both suffer equally.

9 Some French moulters are the birds with the biggest and best head qualities.

10 If the feathers affected are not drawn early and the stumps are retained in the flesh, the wings bleed a great deal around or through the stumps and eventually scar tissue forms, preventing any possibility of normal feathering occurring.

11 Excessive breeding does not cause the disease.

12 The disease is peculiar to parrotlike species only.

The normal feather

Composed of protein, the feathers develop in definite feather tracts all over the body, the base of the feather, the calamus, being contained in its own follicle. These calamuses vary in length, the shorter ones forming the down feathers while these longer ones are the primary and tail feathers. The quill (i.e. the section above the skin level) during growth divides along its length into barbs and in turn the barbs further divide into very fine brush-like barbules. These form the vane of the feather. The calamus has two tiny apertures, one at its tip called the inferior umbilicus and one further up at skin level called the superior umbilicus. During growth the shaft and calamus are filled with blood which feeds the growth of each feather, gradually as the feather attains maximum growth the blood supply ceases and the calamus and shaft harden and become clear. The feather is then firmly anchored and remains in for many months until displaced by the process of moult.

The French moult feather

Growth of affected feathers would appear normal up to the age of three weeks, though almost certainly the feather will be shorter than usual. As the feather reaches maturity the blood supply, instead of being absorbed in the normal way, becomes thick and gelatinous in the region of the superior umbilicus, finally drying within the shaft. The calamus and shaft at that point instead of hardening remain soft and spongy and the calamus becomes narrower at one point much like the neck of a bottle. At this stage the chick is four to five weeks old and it becomes noticeable that the length of the primaries is shorter than usual and that they are loose and lying irregularly. Later still these flights break off and the typical French moult runner irritatingly appears.

The Mite Theory

For many years fanciers were under the impression that an infestation of mites within the confines of the nest box, continually sucking the blood of the chicks, caused a virtual starvation of the feathers during their growth. This is questionable since the problem is confined to parrotlike species and not other varieties of bird which can be equally infected with mite. Plates 15 and 16 of the red mite show quite clearly the mandibles with which the skin of the victim is broken and the blood sucking proboscis is also clearly visible. Seeing this specialized apparatus it would seem a reasonable assumption to blame some species of mite. A variation on this would be to examine in more detail the life cycle of the mites. They reproduce by laying eggs which hatch into a larval form before attaining maturity. It is a reasonable line of thought that as the incidence of French moult is less or non-existent in the first round, when the cages have perhaps been disinfected prior to breeding, then by the second round perhaps thousands of mite eggs have been laid coupled with the fact the warmer weather has encouraged infestation. It may be therefore that the young chick is the preferred laying site of the mites for their eggs and it is conceivable that those eggs are positioned at the base or actually down the shaft of the follicles. It is also important to remember that of the percentage of mites that are visible there are perhaps ten times as many too small to be seen, either due to immaturity or because they are smaller species. Many fanciers have experienced several consecutive years free of French moult when, for some other reason, the aviary has been fumigated annually with sulphur candles.

The Nutrition Theory

In the late 1950s Dr T. G. Taylor of Reading University instituted work on the problem of French moult and for a period of some seven years systematically, under controlled experiments, examined all forms of nutritional deficiencies and excesses without isolating any one factor responsible. To sum up those years of invaluable work is very difficult, but Dr Taylor's conclusions were that a first-class diet containing all the essential vitamins and minerals was the best way to avoid contracting the disease. The research team admitted they were working on birds which were continuously breeding, in an attempt to establish a cause and the scope of the research did not embrace the study of possible cures. Foods containing every nutritional supplement known to be required by birds was given over the period of research to no avail. However one cannot categorically deny that the current theory that an imbalance in the diet may be the cause. Deficiencies and excesses of any one item must be avoided as far as possible in an attempt to prevent this scourge.

Index